D1741021

# ©2018 Grayden Damien

# DISCLAIMER:

This book is a memoir or in other terms an autobiography written by the author. The stories told in this memoir are based off of the author's memories and personal experiences. Some of the events, names, and details may have been changed to protect the privacy of those involved. This is a retelling from the author's perspective and opinions expressed are strictly the author's and may not be representative of that particular event or person. Other details may have been altered for literary effect. This book should be treated as a literary work and is intended for entertainment purposes.

# CHAPTER GUIDE

# ~Making an Entrance~

I should warn you now that this is going to be one hell of a story. If you are reading this I would assume you already know who I am. I can't imagine a scenario where some random stranger would pick this up. Enough rambling! For those of you who may not know me allow me to introduce myself. I started going professionally by, Grayden Damien, I'm an entertainer, model, professional wrestler, and a fun time. I acquired the name Damien when I wrestled for a popular gay pro-wrestling video site called UCW (Underground Championship Wrestling). Grayden was a name I was already known by basically it was an extension of the name, Aiden, which is a nickname and alternate name that some knew me as. Damien is a name that I will explain later when I get to the wrestling chapters of this book. Which brings me to my next point. Why the hell am I writing a book now?

I feel like I have a fascinating story at this point in my life. There is also a lot of things that my fans may not know about me and may be surprised to learn. That and anyone who has followed any part of my career knows that there has been some drama and controversy. I will warn you now that a

1

lot of what I present in this book may piss some people off. This isn't meant to bash anyone or make anyone look bad. I'm not going to drag people through the mud just to embarrass and humiliate them. These are my thoughts and personal opinions. Just because I had a bad experience with someone doesn't mean they are a horrible person. I'm not here to put anyone down but I am going to speak honestly and candidly. Are we on the same page?

With that being said let's take a look at some of the things I will be covering in this book. This is obviously an autobiography of sorts. My life has been controversial and at times really just messed up. I want to give you a behind the scenes look at some of those moments. I will be covering my professional wrestling career, both in the gay wrestling community as well as on the indy scene. There will be aspects of my modeling career that I will share for the first time ever! Things that I've only discussed with those close to me and some things that I never felt comfortable sharing outside of those circles. There will of course be some personal stories which will cover a variety of topics and some of those may shock you as well. Some people may be able to relate to some of the more personal struggles that I've faced. It isn't all drama and controversy. I'm also going to have some fun with this. I mean this is me we are talking about. You know some crazy shit is about to go down!

I'm excited to share this journey with you. I think you're going to be in for quite the treat. At times there will be things that may not make sense or you might be looking at me like, "What the fuck, Grayden Damien?" I assure you by the end of our journey it will come full circle. Get your mind out of the gutter! I know you are thinking of a circle jerk! Actually you probably weren't but now you are. Let's do this! Start the book that is! Not the circle jerk you pervert!

# CHAPTER 1 -Trying to find my place

What should we talk about first? Do you want to know who I hooked up with while wrestling in UCW? Awesome! I will get to that in a later chapter because I don't want to spoil all the good stuff. Why don't we start off with some troubled past shit? Everybody loves that kind of sappy shit, right?

One of the biggest challenges I face is finding my place in the gay community. I don't personally identify as gay, straight, bisexual or anything really. Being involved in the gay entertainment business you would think it would be much easier but it really isn't. I've mentioned similar things in the past. A lot of you know that I was married to a at the time wonderful man. My former husband appeared in a few wrestling videos with me. He has even made a few appearances with me including several of my wrestling birthday parties. Devin is the name he goes by for those who don't already know. I wanted to surprise Devin for his big twenty first birthday. It would be a late celebration but a celebration indeed. A mutual friend of ours who was also one of my best men at our wedding arranged to take us to D.C. for a weekend outing. We were going to be going to a huge gay club in the area which was also a strip club. I had never actually been a customer at a gay strip club in my entire life. I'll get to the other half of that in a bit.

We got to the club and from the moment we got there I was flat out uncomfortable. I got such a seedy vibe from the place and I didn't really want to stay there. I felt like I could catch and STD from just standing there. This is the same reason that I end up missing out on a lot of gay pride events and things of that sort. I just feel like everyone is trying way too hard to act like a total slut and it always has made me feel a bit out of place. This was really no different. I had been to a lot of straight strip clubs and I never felt like they were trashy. I mean there were a few that were complete dive places and had some butt ass ugly women but nothing felt odd. I'm not uncomfortable with nudity in anyway either so it is nothing like that. Something just rubbed me the wrong way! That probably sounds awful the way I just worded that. I don't mean someone rubbed their penis on me in the club although it wouldn't have been the first time. I've dealt with my fair share of creeps.

I walk into the club and of course it is your typical club that is dimly light, smells of rotten cigarette smoke and over-priced booze. I'm looking

5

to see if they have a stage where dancers would be. I figured I could sit in the back and when I get a bit more comfortable move closer to the stage to tip. To my surprise I walk a few more feet and there is a dick in my face. There is just this dude stripping on a speaker. It reminded me of Friday nights at this one gay club I used to frequent. I just thought this dude was a customer and acting like a total slut but no this was one of their strippers. I look around a bit more and all throughout the club there are designated spots where the entertainers are dancing and just basically on the floor with the customers. I just want to sit down and relax and have a few drinks to see if I can get more comfortable but as I walk up to the bar there is a black guy that is performing and sucking his own dick on stage while people place tips in his sock. My anxiety is getting the better of me here. I march on forward doing my best Helen Keller. Seriously! Like I am bumping into tables, people, chairs, helicopter cocks. I blindly lead myself to the bar and then my jaw drops at the insanely high price of the drinks. They also don't have the drink I want but that is ok. I was a fan of some hard ciders and apple ale type of drinks. The bartender suggested this other hard cider to me and I surprisingly never heard of it until that moment. It was called Angry Orchard but I just called it Angry

O because I often switched up the way I pronounced Orchard and didn't want to sound stupid if I ordered it with the wrong name. I seriously had never had one before.

Truth be told I was never a big drinker. I had actually just started to try a few new drinks because my husband turned twenty one and my best friend was going through a break up. This bitch he was dating decided she would lead him on and then made all these excuses as to why she couldn't go out with him after going on several dates with him. Turned out she was seeing another guy at the same time and we ran into them at a fast food place. He took it a lot harder than I expected him. I had known him for a good twenty years and he looked soul crushed. I had never seen him look so distraught. He never talks about his emotions but I could tell this was eating him apart. Just the sight of seeing her with another man was hurting him. He was always a good friend and more like a brother to me and you don't want to see your family hurt like that. I had told him that we could go to the liquor store and get a bottle of Jack and go back to my apartment and have a drinking night to forget about everything.

We so hooked up after! No we really didn't just throwing that out there to see if you were paying attention. We also got a few different malt beverages because I was never a big beer fan and only had malt beverages or a select few hard ciders. In my efforts to make him feel better I ended up getting drunk for the first time ever in my life. I had no idea what that felt like and it felt wonderful. I am sure that is a horrible thing to say but it helped us forget about the wretched bitch.

Back to the seedy gay club here. As I mentioned before I got sidetracked, they don't have my normal hard cider at the bar and I am pissed. The bartender recommends me the Angry O and I fall in love! It tastes so damn amazing to me. I have since fallen in love with a different hard cider but that is natural. Well I end up having a few more drinks and it loosens me up a bit and I am getting a bit more comfortable with the idea of being there. I still think the place is rather off putting but I am not as freaked out as I was. Meanwhile Devin and I are messaging this guy on Grindr who happens to be at the club. He joins us at our table and then of course I go back into defense mode because that is just how I am it seems. He tries to start feeling up our legs and into our pants. I am now doing this awkward fidget to give him a hint and slap his hand away. He then buys us both a drink and I know exactly what he was trying to do. Another drink had loosened me up and I was considering taking him up on his three-way offer but another part of me still had some common sense. He ended up moving on to another guy and probably hooked up with him. My night did get a little better once I had some more alcohol in me. I'll tell you this, when you didn't drink your entire adult life the first few times it feels like a magic potion. Once we got our ride back to our hotel I did some reflecting. I was reminded of why exactly that place freaked me out so much. My friend was going on about how a lot of the dancers would go back to hotels with people and have sex with them. Our friend was telling us this story of how he is friends with one of the dancers and some of the things he does. This dancer is not afraid to make some extra money out of club hours and that is something that hit me a bit hard. I had almost all but forgotten some of the horrible experiences I had when I was eighteen and working at a gay club. Time for a bit of a flashback here!

I had just turned eighteen and it seemed like a lot of interesting offers were coming my way. It was something that overwhelmed me and nothing that I expected. I never really thought I was overly good looking. I knew I had some handsome features and a few people found me attractive but I never considered myself hot. All throughout my school days I was very active and into all sorts of athletics even though I was far from a typical jock. I did wrestling, basketball, running, and soccer for a bit. Eventually I just stopped giving a fuck and hanging out with social rejects. The troubled teens were whom I related with. I wasn't wanting to mimic their behaviour but I knew the feeling of not belonging. A new crowd of people brought a change in my personality and some health issues to go with it. There was a period of time where I battled body issues. I always felt too thin or too fat depending on what the scale said. If the perfect number wasn't there I'd either stop eating or eat more.  I really just wanted people to notice me and to be liked. I let it drive me into a monstrous depression. I started to hang out at gay clubs in an attempt connect with the local gay community. I didn't have much confidence because of the body issues I faced previously. I would eventually meet someone at a club that helped me work on my confidence issues. Was a guy that I connected with and started dating. He was the ideal guy. I put him on a pedestal of superlative perfection. He was pale, slim, shaggy brown hair, incredible blue eyes, chiseled jawline and very much out of my league. I remember being at the club with my best friend, Nikki. She saw me transfixed on this guy. She said, "Go dance with him." I was trying to figure out any excuse in my head to say no but I couldn't even really think of how to respond. "He's not here with anyone, he's been looking this way a few times. You got this go out there and get his attention. I'll come with you." I don't know why I was stupid enough to believe her. She did come with me and she started to dance with me up next to him. I don't exactly know what happened next but she squeezed herself into the middle of us. We were at the point where she was making herself look like a whore and grinding against the both of us. In a matter of minutes she just vanishes off with some random guy and here I am with this total stranger feeling awkward.

"I'm Cayden, your friend is a good dancer." I reply, "Thanks, I'm sorry about her she has this idea in her head that you were checking me out. That is so silly though." I don't know what the hell I just said. I'm thinking I just made an absolute fool out of myself but he comes back with, "I was! All night actually. I'm glad she brought you over because I was too shy and nervous to approach you. You are really cute. Do you mind staying to dance with me?"

I had No idea he saw in me but he made me feel attractive. I soon found myself hanging out with him every few days and then staying over his place on the weekends. One of the nights at the club he was dancing with me and he comes in closer and embraces me. I feel him caressing my hair and rubbing his other hand up and down my back under my shirt. He then starts to kiss me and my world starts spinning. I got bewildered in the trance music and strobe lights. I kiss him back and I push my tongue into his mouth while I rub my hands on his body under his shirt. He undoes my shirt and starts to pull it off and I do the same to him. Now here we are both eighteen standing in this club shirtless in an embrace skin to skin. His body heat feels magnetic and I can't pull myself away. I was totally comfortable in a situation I'd normally be panicked in. I didn't care if others were staring at my body or what they might think of how gross I looked or didn't look. I had him holding me and everything just felt right.

Our relationship didn't last long. I just felt the timing wasn't right for me to be in a serious relationship which is where it seemed like it was heading. I was young and eighteen and wanted to explore my options. He helped bring me out of my depression and I started to feel better about myself. I am not sure I could have done that without him there. It gave me a new confidence that others took notice in. This is when those interesting offers started to come up. Here I was basically your typical twink. I had a slim figure and of course a nice cock that everybody wanted a piece of. I put myself out there on social networks and gay dating sites. I had Nikki take alluring photos of me and plastered them all over my profile. Photos of me in just my underwear, fresh out of the shower in just a towel, relaxing in bed, or in designer clothes that I bought at the thrift store. I wanted to put myself out there and see what would happen. People started to respond as I built up my friends list. I would get messages of "Daddies" looking for a nice "Twink" to spoil. You know the typical shit that comes with that when you have just become legal. I ended up networking with two rather interesting people. One was a gay porn producer and the other was the owner of a gay club that was looking for help. I'll start with the gay club owner.

This was not the normal club I went to and this was in regards for a new club. I didn't really know much of what to expect because anytime I went to the club I never paid attention to the staff.

This guy reached out to me and needed help with promoting his club and someone attractive to work the floor. I really had no idea what that meant but I was young and dumb and the job seemed like it would be vapid enough that a monkey could do it. Little did I know what the hell I was about to get myself into.

The club owner Rob had found me via one of the social media sites that I was using at the time. We had exchanged a few messages prior to me even knowing he had a club. One thing that bothered me about a lot of people that were my age was how narrow-minded they were. I hated hanging out with gay guys my own age because they would shut out anyone over the age of twenty two. I was being nice enough to talk to this guy who wasn't even forty yet. Rob was reasonably good looking but not really a catch. He was somewhere in his mid-thirties and slightly overweight but not obsese. He was clean shaven and had dirty blonde hair that was slightly combed over to hide a receding hair line. He had seemed very easy going and didn't just want to get in my pants. I enjoyed getting compliments from strangers and he never came off to be some sort of freakish creep. We had exchanged messages for a few days and then he told me about this new gay club that he had just opened. He arranged to meet me at a local diner for a "business lunch" that he would pay for and he could get to know me a bit better and basically interview me for the position.

The lunch was very professional. He never talked to me in a way that could be sexually inappropriate or seem eccentric. He went over some of what I would be doing and some of the things he hoped I would be comfortable doing. Things like some light cleaning, refilling ice, restocking soda, taking customer orders for appetizers and light kitchen work. He asked me how I felt about working in my underwear. I had done a few "underwear contests" at the other gay club when I was with Cayden, but I wasn't sure how I could do it without him. I didn't want to reach out to Cayden and have him steal what could be an interesting opportunity for me to expose myself (no pun intended) and get myself out there to other opportunity.  I had questioned him because I wasn't sure how that lined up with everything else he was describing. I didn't realize the club used to be a strip club and still had a shower stage, stripper poles, runway stage and not much remodeling had been done since the strip club closed down. He was telling me that I would just be "performing" on occasion in my underwear and that there would be no nudity required just some erotic seduction. I wasn't really sure what that all meant but for one reason or another I trusted him and agreed to be a performer. A monotone generic ringtone soon interrupted our business meeting. It was his business partner who acted as the assistant manager to the place. He was driving through the area and Rob told him to stop by and meet me.

A few minutes of casual conversation passed by and I had almost all but forgotten that we were even in a business meeting. In walks another guy in hid mid-thirties Italian-Jewish looking guy. He had short jet black hair slightly greased back, rounder face, and somewhat of an angry looking unibrow. He dressed in darker clothing that was slightly beat up looking and a pair of ripped jeans and pointy toed shoes. He had on a generic cool water cologne and introduced himself as, Ken. I did not get the same vibe from him that I got from Rob. Ken had this arrogant prescience to him and he was a lot harder to figure out. I couldn't tell if he was trying to hard to be cool or if he was just an asshole. Meeting Ken almost made me say no to the job and looking back on that day I probably should have. I was desperate for work as I wasn't getting many hours at the job I was working and I could benefit from having extra money as I was looking ahead to travel to Ireland at some point. Rob told me that Ken would be picking me up for my first weekend of work.

It came time to the weekend and it was nearing time for Ken to pick me up. I walked to the designated meeting spot because I did not want Ken to know where I lived because I didn't get a good vibe from him. Ken picks me up in a black Dodge pickup truck. The club was only a twelve mile drive from where we were and the first few minutes of said drive were awkward. I am naturally shy around new people and even shyer when I don't feel comfortable around somewhere. He was asking me some probing questions about my relationship and different personal things. I responded with mostly lies that made me sound tougher than I was. The drive goes on without any issues and Ken almost seems less creepy but I still get an odd sense from him.

I walk into the club and the place looks incredible. Neon rope lights are running along the catwalk part of the stage. There is shiny gold string curtain where "performers" come out from. The shower part of the stage has 4 shower heads for multiple performers to get wet and wild. The seating areas are velvet purple and dark colors. It almost looks like a more royal and slightly classy establishment. Rob takes me to a small storage room which is the "dressing rob" he has a box of underwear that he wants me to try on. Being as pale as I am I go for some darker colored underwear that don't flush my skin out and don't conceal my package. He tells me that for the first part of my night I'd just be walking around in a polo and some dress pants and as the night progresses that I could start to strip down. Part of my job details involve hanging around the customers and striking up friendly conversation and being flirty and even dancing on them if I have to.

The first hour passes and the club was mostly dead. Finally the late evening crowd starts to pour in and here is my big moment. I go into the dressing room and take off my clothes and change into some purple thin strapped underwear. They are low rise and have about of inch of material on the back covering my ass crack. I walk around with my pen and notepad to see if anyone in the club wants to order anything. As I walk out I have a few guys staring at me. Part of me feels like I shouldn't welcome the attention but the other part of me feels like I finally feel comfortable enough to deserve that kind of attention. I go up to and find a few guys who are over forty and strike up a conversation with them. Most of them are married men and just like coming to gay clubs to escape from their reality. I sit between the two macho guys of the group and wrap my arms around them. They both instantly are glued to me and rub their hands over my chest and down towards my well-toned swimmer like abs. I'm getting slightly turned on by this myself which I think to myself can't be a good thing. I get up from between them and start dancing seductively. They soon both pull out twenty dollar bills and stick them in my underwear. I'm like "Wow that was super easy!" I leave to walk around the club and talk to some other customers. I had to do a dance routine on stage at Midnight. I am freaking out over that because now I am no longer talking to people one on one I am the center of attention. I've always performed really well in front of an audience but this was the first time I had to be "sexy" for an audience. I perform to two or three songs and guys are throwing one dollar bills on the stage and waving them around for me to come their way. I seductively start to partially remove my underwear with my thumbs interlocked in the straps. Just enough to expose my pubic hair I can't fully remove them since I was told we weren't doing full nude yet. The guys in the crowd seem delighted and I feel like I'm the sexiest guy in the world. All of that hard work and I hadn't had a chance to pee. I make my way to the bathroom and encounter the two guys that I danced for earlier in the night.

Here they are in the bathroom and one had the other's erect cock in his mouth. This guy is getting a blowjob and I walk in on this and have no idea what the hell is going on or what I'm supposed to do. They just glance at me for a second and the guy continues to suck him off. I turn around to walk back out the door and the one guy says "wait a minute, you can get in on this to I can jack you off while he sucks me off and he can suck your dick too." I am speechless and appalled and don't know what to do. I just come up with some lame ass excuse as to why I can't "I was coming in to clean the bathroom. I can't stay in here too long or my boss will come looking for me!" I'm like hell yeah that sounds awesome in my head. I go to walk out the door and I hear "TWO HUNDRED DOLLARS! I'll give you two hundred dollars right now if you come over here and let me jack you off. Five hundred if you want to put on a condom and fuck me in the ass." I don't even say anything at this point and just walk out of the bathroom and try to pretend as if the whole thing didn't just happen. I obviously did not take them up on their offer because I could not see myself doing that. Part of me was thinking that five hundred dollars was a good amount of money for about twenty minutes of work but I had morals and I wasn't that desperate for money. The rest of my night I tried to just block all of that out of my mind. I also attempt to avoid those two guys any chance I got. Thankfully I succeeded and it was time for Ken to take me home. At this point in time Ken is looking like a saint compared to these two nutcases.

Being shaken up by the events of the night I just don't feel much like in a talking mood. I probably look like an even bigger asshole than before but I try to look at the positives. I made really good tips and aside from the two weirdos I had a good night. Things would get a lot more interesting as the weeks progressed. Now it was time for them to hire more people and this is where this place started to become more and more of a circus.

The following weekend I would be introduced to new staff. This particular weekend saw the club hire three very diverse individuals. First up was Kyle, he resembled an alien mixed with a monkey but he was in incredibly amazing shape.

He had also been very popular on some of the social networking sites and he could use to promote the club. From a business stand point I saw why it was important to bring him on board. He had thousands of friends, while I only had a few hundred. He would be an incredible asset with an incredible ass! I actually rarely interacted with him because he was over the top gay in my opinion. I figured we would have little in common but he was connected and being friends with him could get me places so I at least would be friendly. Next up was probably the biggest douchebag I had ever had the displeasure of meeting. I honestly have no idea what Rob saw in him or what he could bring to the club. This guy to me had a revolting personality and wasn't even that good looking. He isn't even worth describing! He is the kind of guy that thinks he should be in an underwear catalog or preppy clothing model but aside from the ego doesn't have the looks to back it up. This guy's name was, Stefan. When he introduced himself he was talking like he was a supervisor and how we should address him and that we were basically peasants under him. As long as he stayed out of my way and wasn't a burden I wouldn't make a big deal out of it. The last guy brought in for that weekend was incredibly gorgeous and allegedly "straight." I had a bit of an

instant crush on him. Kyle and Stefan were both
over twenty-one but Travis was eighteen like me,
but way out of my league. He resembled somewhat
of a Roman God and had incredibly wavy blonde
surfer hair and pouty luscious full lips. I couldn't
keep my eyes off him.

I wanted to get to know Travis a bit better.
Not just because he was the most gorgeous man I
had ever laid my eyes on, but because out of the
three new hires he wasn't a douchebag. Luckily I
would be assigned to help train him so he would be
shadowing me around. The first night working with
Travis meant I joked around with him and got him
to laugh and most everything I would say. He
thought I was cool and funny but he had no idea
how much I wanted to just be with him. He told me
he was nervous about performing for gay men. He
had really needed money as he had just lost his
father and his mother was struggling to pay the
bills. He felt that he had hit a low point. I told him to
come to the dressing room with me and we could
talk in private as this was a conversation best not to
be out in the open. I put my feelings aside and just
went into protective mode. I gave him a hug and
just let him cry on my shoulder. I rubbed his back
and comforted him and the thought of attempting

anything with him didn't even cross my mind. I just wanted to make sure he was ok but I also realized his situation and had to give him some real talk. I told him, "that it wasn't going to be easy and it might tear at you emotionally at times especially if you are a straight male. There will be times you just want to run away and hide but you have to be strong. You have to go out there and be ruthless and be in control and show these guys that you own them. These guys will pick up on your vulnerability and exploit it to their advantage." I really had no idea what I was talking about because I hadn't even been performing very long myself. I was good at reading people and situations and that is how I perceived this job. When he went out on stage later to dance for the guys. He went out there with such confidence and he looked incredible doing it. As the weeks progressed our working relationship would get more intense as would my relationship with my other co-workers but not in a good way.

Kyle was starting to act a bit strange towards me. The more I worked with him the more awkward things got. Little did I know that he was blowing Stefan on "breaks" in the dressing room. Stefan was also spreading nasty rumors about me for no apparent reason. I had overheard him say some awful things about me. He would go around telling customers that if I talked to them it would just be because I wanted them to give me money to suck their dick behind the dumpster. He would tell customers that I was secretly straight and bringing my girlfriend in to fuck in customer's cars that I would pretend to valet park. Stupid things that really made no sense. He was just a bully for no reason and I didn't even want to bother to get to the root of the situation. He wasn't worth my effort. The thing that pissed me off was he was trying to turn Kyle against me for no reason. Travis also had an odd feeling about Stefan and Stefan would try to then tell Travis rumors about me that just simply weren't true. Travis was dealing with his own issues and honestly didn't need the drama.

The club was going to be introducing shower dancing the following weekend and Stefan was even more pissed that I got selected to be on the advertisement. He let Kyle blow him in the dressing room and then Kyle went home early. Stefan called his boyfriend to bitch and moan about me. I was outside the dressing room and heard the whole thing.

"I can't believe he is on the damn flyer. He looks fucking retarded like his mother fucked her brother."

"He's so fucking nasty, probably only has this job because Rob, feels sorry for him and didn't want him to cut himself"

At first I was hurt, because I never had anyone say anything that negative about me in my entire life. The other thing is if you have a problem with me why not approach me? He continued to go on about how ugly I was and about more shit he was planning on making up about me. I had finally had enough and stormed into the room. Without saying any words I just grabbed his flip phone snapped it half and threw the two pieces against the wall in opposite corners of the room.

"Dude what the fuck was that for?"
"Cut the shit, Stefan! I've heard the shit you have been saying and now I'm confronting you face to face and you have nowhere to go."
"Seriously, I never said anything about you. I don't like you enough to waste my breath uttering your name, whatever the fuck it is."
"I'm not a fucking idiot, Stefan. First of all would you like me to tell Kyle about your boyfriend or are you planning on doing that. Secondly keep away from Travis. He is dealing with enough shit. I know you have been planning to go after him when you

are finished trying to wreck me. This isn't petty High School drama. You fucking say what you have to say to my face and deal with it like an adult."
"I have no idea what you are talking about. Get the hell out of the dressing room you fucking ugly ass inbred" The next thing you know he slaps me across the face.

I had finally had enough of pretending that we could talk this over like adults. I have no idea what came over me but before he could say anything else I just cock my arm back, curl my fist and deliver him a knockout punch across the face. He falls back into the leather chair and I slowly back out of the room. He gets up and runs toward me and attempts to swing at me. I duck down and get low to thrust my shoulder into him. I knee him in the stomach, then maneuver myself around him and have his arm locked up take him down to the ground. I now have him positioned in a way where it is hard for him to escape, but if he had any wrestling experience, or basic mma skills he might figure out the easy reversal. Luckily for me he doesn't.

"You fancy yourself quit the bully don't you, Stefan? Look at you now on the ground all helpless with nowhere to run. Seriously don't fuck with me! I will wreck your ass then fuck your father for fun." I got up and gave him a swift kick to the balls to show I wasn't fucking around. "What the fuck man! Alright I'm sorry, Dude!" Stefan uttered with shame. I extended Stefan my hand to help him up. His apology wasn't anywhere close to sincere but I can tell that I gave him a good scare. I walked out of the room and Rob was standing outside. Luckily he hadn't heard any of the commotion that was going on. He says, "Glad to see you two getting to know each other a bit better. You two will be performing in the shower together next weekend. I think you two will be an erotic duo." What the fuck! I just kicked this guys ass and now we have to shower together. I had a feeling that shit was about to get even more insane.

# CHAPTER 2 – The drama continues

The motley emotions that were running through my head for the following week was spiking my anxiety. After the physical confrontation Stefan and I didn't exchange any words, glances, or acknowledged each other. Ken did his best effort to pretend he was concerned about my well being. He felt that something was going on with me and on the drive home following the fight he tried to get it out of me. I went into high defense mode because I still didn't trust Ken and my intuition in these situations is rarely wrong.

"What's going on with you?"

"What do you mean, Ken?"

"Are you having an issue with the club?"

"I'm fine! I just have a headache and need to get home to sleep.", I nervously reply.

"Well you know you can always come back to my place and I can give you a deep massage." *Ken slides his hand onto my lap, slowly inching towards my crotch* "It could help you relax and there is no pressure for a full release."

I go as to if I am reaching in my pocket for my phone and smack his hand away. "Thanks but I just want to get home and relax. No offense but I'm just not in that kind of mood."

It seemed as though Ken was a bit frustrated and defeated and got silent himself until he dropped me off at our meet spot. I just couldn't process everything that had just happened. Was Ken trying to take advantage of me? Do I tell Rob about this? Then there was the whole drama surrounding the fight. How the hell was I ever going pretend that there was no tension between Stefan and I? I was at the point where I just wanted to quit and put the whole thing behind me. I wanted to but I remembered that I took this job to get some much needed extra money and I couldn't walk away from it yet. Plus I wanted to get to know more about Travis and work was our best chance to get to know one another. I couldn't throw in the towel yet but I really wanted to.

As the week progressed and the days got closer to my shower performance with Stefan, more fuel was being added to the fire of drama. Stefan had been posting about me on his blog. He was telling his followers that I was trying to sabotage his career at work and he's just gonna throw me out of the shower. Dude I just basically kicked your ass and you are gonna throw me out of the shower? I wanted to come up with some kind of plan to make myself look like the better person and come out on top of this even stronger. I wasn't sure what that was going to be yet but I just couldn't let Stefan get the upper hand. It was time to play on his level. I was going to upstage him by being a bigger bitch. I was ready to play dirty. I had called my best friend, Nikki. We arranged to meet up later in the day to go to the erotic lingerie and adult shop that a lot of drag queens, adult entertainers, and other kinky people shopped at. While I waited for that I decided to fire back with a blog of my own. I wrote a blog post to fire shots of my own. I felt that this guy needed to know what kind of scum his boyfriend was. Fuck it I wanted enemies so I threw in a few lies for fun. The blog no longer exists because I closed out my Myspace or whatever the hell it was when the site lost popularity but I kept a backup of my blogs because I'm sentimental like that.

*"Have you guys heard? I'm getting tossed out of a shower this weekend. I know I am excited too! It is funny how a shower can symbolize the cleansing of a person. The irony here is that you are one hell of a dirty bastard. It seems that you forgot to tell Kyle that you had a boyfriend? He didn't get the memo. He just posted a bunch of shots of you and him making out at the club. I didn't even have to tell your boyfriend that you make out with co-workers and guys that come to the club and suck*

*their dicks within minutes of meeting them. How many times have you gone on a smoke break to blow some dude behind the dumpster or in the back seat of his car? Meanwhile your boyfriend is loyal to your dumb ass for some reason or another. You made up all this shit about me meanwhile it was stuff that you were actually doing but wanted to make yourself look like a saint. Get the fuck out of here. You can try to toss me out of the shower but I'm gonna work my ass off to give our customers the best show they can. In the process I might give your nasty ass a spanking."*

I don't know what I was thinking with the blog post but it was good to get things out to the open and actually set the rumors straight. Little did I know the drama that would follow.

Nikki, picked me up and we went to the erotic fashion store. I had never been in such a place and was blown away by all the different types of outfits they had for men and women. I was so far removed from any of the gay community or any of the kink and fetish stuff. Nikki and I joked about the harness and leash sets and how that would be fun to incorporate into the shower. "Can you even get leather wet? Will it like melt or something?" Nikki asked. We walked around the store for a bit and got to the kinky men's underwear. I had found these incredibly revealing and sexy mesh-like, slightly see thru, underwear. They were black and orange and just were going to look incredible on me. I managed to find a similar color top. I had planned to rip that off of me after it got soaped and soaked to make the men want me. Just as we were getting ready to check out we hear the gayest shrill coming from across the store. It was Stefan's boyfriend and he was about to bitch slap us into next week. This guy was a well known drag queen and couldn't be any more gay if he tried. I just pictured Rupaul performing an exorcism to let his inner bitch flow through. We had no idea who he was until he was all up in our face.

"Why the hell did you write that fucking blog?"
I was confused because he didn't introduce himself. He was continuing to bitch and causing a huge scene in the store. Everyone around us was looking over in his direction as he flailed his hands and arms as if he was a unicorn shitting rainbows. I was starting to walk away because I didn't want to get involved in this shit. All of a sudden he tries to slap me but Nikki steps in and grabs his wrist with a vice grip and a high heel that was nearby in the other hand.

"Shut the fuck up and stop bitching at us about your fucking whore of a boyfriend. If you don't shut up I will shove this heel down your throat. I was gonna shove it up your ass but you probably already do that on your own time!" Nikki screams out.

Nikki continued to basically degrade him and then tell him about how his boyfriend was whoring around and that he should be mad with him and that us. He wasn't getting it and exclaiming that Stefan loves him and that we are such horrible people. The shop owner ended up coming over and kicked the boyfriend out and apologized to us because he was a repeat problem customer. We got offered a discount and then preceded on our way. Nikki had a surprise in store for me. She was taking me to a tanning salon to get an all over spray tan. We were really pulling out all the stops for this one. I won't bore you with the details of the tanning experience instead I'll flash forward to my big performance night.

Ken came to pick me up and I was getting more anxious as we got closer to the club. Part of me was nervous because I had no idea what Stefan was planning on doing. I was thinking a lot of worst case scenarios. I also had his crazy boyfriend putting me on the top of his shit list. I didn't know if I was going to end up getting jumped by a gaggle of drag queens or what the hell was going to happen. I just had a feeling that the night was going to be one to remember.

We arrive at the club and I go into the dressing room to get changed and walk in on Travis getting changed. I hadn't really seen him full on naked up to this point and only ever really changed with him on opposite sides of the room.

"Oh my God I am so sorry. Do you want me to leave while you finish?"

"No dude! You are fine. If you were Stefan, or Kyle I'd just kick you in the nuts."

His joke made me laugh and we started talking about recent events in our lives. I started to get undressed in front of him and as I took my clothes off he started rubbing his cock and slightly getting erect. I didn't say anything to him about it but I couldn't take my eyes off of it even though I kept trying.

"If I need help getting turned on for the guys later tonight do you want to help me?" Travis asked.

I had no idea how to even respond to that. I slightly brushed it off and dodged the question and started talking about some other things. After the slightly awkward conversation we both went out to the floor to wait on some customers and see if they wanted to order anything or danced for them for some easy tips. We both head back to the back room and Rob is freaking out.

"Where the fuck is Kyle and Stefan!" Rob screams out!" I start thinking that maybe they quit and that was the best news I heard all day. I ask him what's going on and he tells me that they never showed up and we are getting busy and we have a show to also deliver to the customers. I jokingly told him to check the parking lot in case he was blowing someone. Rob didn't really appreciate the joke but thought it was a good idea because he apparently was well aware of some of the things Stefan did. The next thing you know Rob is heading out the door and Kyle comes rushing in saying he needs to use the phone to call for an ambulance. Evidently Stefan overdosed on something in the parking lot. I am not sure what it was and it was really none of my business. Kyle says that he can't work now and Rob is freaking out even more. Rob looks at Travis and tells him that he is now going to put us together in the shower.

I'm both excited and beyond nervous about this because I couldn't stop thinking of how I saw him earlier in the night. Part of my fantasy was now coming true but how the hell was I going to compose myself enough. I didn't want to look like I was in the later stages of Parkinson's Disease with how badly I felt the urge to shake. I tried not to think too much on it because I wanted to remain professional and just do my job. It was almost time for our performance and I was about to have a full blown panic attack. To my surprise Nikki actually had shown up to watch my show. She was concerned when she didn't see Stefan or Kyle in the club. I ran into her as I was about to go on stage with Travis.

"You made it! What the hell am I gonna do I have to get in the shower with Travis?"
"Oh My God! You are so lucky but does he know you like him?"
"Nikki, I think he wanted me to suck his dick. He was rubbing himself asking me to help him get turned on for the guys tonight?"
"That is so strange. He is either playing with your emotions or he just wants to get some. You know what? Fuck it! These people want a show. Give them the show of your life. Push your boundaries and tease the fuck out of Travis in the process. This way you can get him on the edge of busting a nut and there will be twice as much passion and then probably more tips. So go for it!"

Nikki was right. I had to make this performance count. I gave her a hug and went to go calm myself down and it was show time. Travis walked out to the shower first and did his own little dance number to the delight of the crowd. Then whoever the DJ was that night asked the crowd over the erotic trance music if they wanted more. The crowd of course erupted and that was my cue to go to stage. Here I am in my see thru shirt and my perfectly picked out underwear. I get over to the shower area and awkwardly start to grind up on Travis. The chemistry I had hoped for was sort of on the lackluster side and I needed to think of something fast to not get booed out of the building. I got under the water stream and my shirt started to get wet. I turned around and faced directly in front on Travis and he was already down to his underwear from his solo performance. We rubbed against each other underwear to underwear and started and reached toward the hanging loofah sponge and stated to soap him up. I got closer to him and told him to slowly rip off my shirt and then start to lick my chest and work your way down to my crotch. He was slightly confused and started to whisper in my ear as he slightly nibbled on it to hide our conversation from the audience. I would do the same to him to give him further instructions.

"What do you mean?"

"When I was in the back I cut a slit in my shirt. If you rip it down the middle water will pour down my chest and look erotic and sexy. If you start to tease me the crowd will want me to tease you back. We will make so much money in the tip jar. Just trust me on this one."

"Don't get me too excited or we will have to finish this after the show in private."

I again blocked out his obvious come on and he continued to do as instructed. He ripped open my shirt and started to rub my chest and then he started to lick from my chest down to my abdomen. He got to my navel and started licking down that area. That got me quivering as I wasn't aware of how sensitive that area was on me. He went further down and started to rub his face in my bulge. I was getting quite the obvious erection and he was teasing the fuck out of me through my underwear. I grab him by his hair and pull him up towards me as he licks up my body. We start to make out and then I lick him in the same seductive manner that he just licked me. I go down to his underwear and start to pull them down a little. Just enough to get a sneak peak but not reveal the whole package. I turn him around with his rear end facing the audience and continue to pull his underwear down a bit more. With his rear end exposed I rub my face in his crotch and take a lick or two. Then I pull his underwear backup but I keep my hands underneath them. He then sticks his hands in my underwear doing the same. We are essentially rubbing each other under our underwear and the crowd is loving us. We hear over the club speakers for the crowd to make some noise for us. Our cue to end our performance. We head back to the dressing room.

"Travis, that was quite an awesome performance. I can't wait to see what we made in tips. Guys were throwing dollars in that tip bucket left and right."

He didn't even respond to my statement and I thought I had done something to piss him off but to my surprise he pushed me back down on the couch and mounts himself on top of me.

"We need to finish this."
He pushes me back and starts to kiss me in the same way that he did in the shower. I give in and just go with it. Just like in the shower he starts licking down towards my crotch but this time since we are in private he actually pulls out my cock and starts to give me a blowjob. I run my fingers through his hair

as he is blowing me and the excitement of it all has me almost ready to just cum in his mouth. I pull him back and tell him to let me take over. I honestly didn't want to get off too soon. We switch positions and I am the one who ends up starting to blow him. I go back up towards his mouth as I am sitting on top of him. I am now rubbing up against his erect cock with my butt. I tease his cock a bit with that rubbing and I slowly start to straddle. I told him to "fuck me". I slowly start to sit back on his cock but as I do I hear someone on the other side of the door and I jump off and grab my towel and tell him to cover up as well. Surprise! It was Rob on the other side of the door and he came in and just the worst possible moment. I don't think he saw anything that was going on but I played it cool anyway.

"Wanted to tell you guys that you did an awesome job tonight. You made the most tips out of any of the performances yet! We will have to book you guys together in another show."

Then for some reason he decided to update us on Stefan as if we even cared. He let us know that Stefan had accidentally overdosed on some sort of perception drug and he was currently getting treated at the hospital. It looked like he was going to be just fine. It was that time for me to go home. Ken looked way too happy to take me home but since Nikki was there, I decided to ride with her. Ken looked pissed off. Little did I know that he had something up his sleeve and I was next on his list.

## CHAPTER 3 – I'm not gonna fuck the boss

I had returned the following weekend to the club in one of the most gleeful moods I had ever been in. I was on the verge of having some sort of relationship with Travis. Even if it was just a purely sexual one and nothing else I at least was fulfilling a fantasy of mine. At the same time I started to feel like a bit of a scum. I mean I was going after a guy who was dealing with a lot of personal shit and was vulnerable at times. I wasn't sure how much of it was actually him wanting to have something with me or him just looking for an escape from reality.

Kyle wasn't back yet because he claimed there was some sort of emotional damage and Stefan was out of the hospital but evidently looking to seek some sort of treatment for his drug problem. I had looked forward to seeing Travis, but it had seemed he had come down with some sort of illness and was throwing up the entire weekend. So then I was just sort of the only guy working that night so I had to really just haul some ass on everything I was doing. Ken was following me around all night but I couldn't for the life of me figure out why. He seemed to be more infatuated with me than ever.

Rob had made some rather off the wall remarks about how he wish he could have seen Travis and I do some more stuff together. He was hinting at the idea of Travis and I doing some sort of video work together. His comments didn't really bother me as it seemed more business oriented and less perverted but man was there something odd up with Ken.

Ken started talking to me about how I should come over to his place and we can get to know each other a bit better and that he would love to give me a massage because of how tense I looked lately. I was getting the strangest vibe from him and it was making me very uncomfortable. I told him that I had some work that I needed to get done. He told me that he wanted to see me later before the night was over. He can discuss giving me a raise. I wasn't sure what any of that meant. I just wanted to get out of there. I called Nikki to see what she was up to. Sadly she was stuck working because her store was doing something with inventory or some sort of sale. So she was unable to come out because she was working late. So now I was going to be stuck there the rest of the night. I just had to figure out how I was going to avoid Ken. Especially when he was going to be my ride home. I pretended to be doing some work but snuck into the office when nobody was looking to look at a phone book. I was looking up a number for a taxi service to see if there were any in the area. I had found a few taxi services but most of them weren't even doing overnight service. Especially with me being where I was. They weren't going to waste the gas to drive out all that way.

I carried on with my night and was thinking of talking to Rob about doing the video work with Travis. I really wanted to know more about what it would be. I didn't know if Travis would even be on board but I liked the idea and I really wanted something to happen between Travis and I.

It had been a while since I even had interacted with some sleazy patrons but there must have been something in the water that night. This one older gentleman started chatting me up. At first I was thinking nothing of it as I was used to some older guys hitting on me and at times I liked the attention. It made me feel like I was attractive, when at times I had the worst confidence issues. I think when you are young and eighteen like that you don't realize how often people can exploit your vulnerability to their advantage. I feel in a lot of ways at that time I felt older than I was. I was a lot more intuitive and just more perceptive to things that others weren't. Anyway this guy wanted to also take me home but wanted to "keep me". I am not quite sure what that meant but I knew it didn't sound like something I would be up to. He kept telling me how I could live the lavish lifestyle and have anything I want. I also would be allowed to be naked whenever I wanted and he would never force me to wear clothes. I didn't have time for that kind of bullshit so I moved on and just tried to make the best out of what was turning out to be quite a miserable night. For once I would be thrilled if Stefan was there just so I had someone to make fun of or at least recommend to the creeps that were interacting with me.

My suspicions of a bizarre night were continuing to flourish. I couldn't shake the feeling of something not right. When it came time for me to entertain the crowd, I just completely lacked the enthusiasm. I reluctantly danced and I couldn't feel the music, and I think the crowd could tell because I was barely making any tips. Rob was nowhere to be found so he wasn't even watching my disappointing showing. Ken was watching and practically foaming at the mouth. After my performance he wanted to see me in the office. I was at this point just hoping maybe I would be getting fired and could focus on doing other things. I didn't let my guard down and just assumed that this had to be something work related. I still had that suspicion in the back of my mind that this man was a slime ball and up to something but surely he couldn't be? Could he?

"So I'd like to talk to you, about some things. Is that ok?"

"Ken, if it is about my performance tonight. I felt it was an off night for me. I was worried about Travis since he wasn't feeling well."

"What are you talking about? Your performance was incredible as always. It really got me going."

"What do you mean?"

"I just think with a performance like that I think you owe it to me to give me a private performance right now. I can really make it worth it for you."

All the feelings I had going throughout the night seemed to all come to a climax here. It seemed like Ken was propositioning me in one way or another. I was at the point where I was beyond uncomfortable. I really didn't know what to say or what to even do. I just knew that if I didn't think fast I would be in a place that I may not have wanted to be in.

"Ken, I am not quite sure what you are trying to do here. I'd like to keep things between us on a professional level. So if you'll excuse me I am going to be leaving for the night."

I wasn't quite sure what I was going to do because I had no ride home but I figured I would probably figure something out on the way. As I was getting up to leave Ken grabs my arm and pulls me back towards him.

"Don't fight it. I know that this is what you want." Ken says to me

Before I could make my next move Ken shoves me into the wall and forces himself on me. I'm now pinned up against the wall with him holding my arms drilled into the wall. I wasn't sure what the hell I was going to do at this point. This guy is much bigger and much stronger than I am. I was in a really bad situation and my only hope was that someone would walk in. I couldn't really scream for help because who the hell would hear me with as loud as the music was. Ken starts to rub his crotch into me and I can feel him getting erect through his pants. The feeling was not mutual at all and I was limp as could be.

He releases one of his hands off my arms but pivots his body to keep me pinned to the wall. He starts to unzip his pants and then lets them leisurely fall to the floor. He wasn't wearing underwear so now he is not wearing pants, completely erect and gets me back into the first pinned positioned. I wasn't quite sure what he had in mind at this point but I knew it couldn't be good. Was he going to try to fuck me? Make me suck his dick? I didn't want any part of that. I don't know what made me do my next course of action but I started to play along. I was pretending that I was about ready to submit. He loosened his grip on my arms a bit and as soon as he did I saw my opening. I take my knee and give the hardest possible thrust into his groin area. He immediately hunches over in pain and completely releases his grip. Whatever adrenaline rush I had I used full force as I went into linebacker mode and charged myself at him knocking him into the office desk. I now knew at this point that it was one of those fight or flight type situations and I had already made things worse. I start heading towards the office door he starts getting up. I drop to the ground because I noticed there was a hammer on the floor. I pick up the hammer, get back up onto my feet. Now I at least have something I could use if I had to defend myself. I tell him to get the fuck back and I'm not afraid to use this. I walk backwards towards the door. He still has pants down and as I'm about to make my exit I run into Rob.

Now Rob is blocking my exit and in my mind I am thinking this could be some sort of set up. I just had to get out of there because at that point I don't know if Rob had something planned and was waiting for Ken to loosen me up. Rob asked what was going on when he noticed that Ken had his pants down and me with a hammer. I am not sure how that must of looked or what kind of fetish he thought was involved. I tell him to get the hell out of my way and Ken was a fucking slime ball. Rob started yelling at Ken but I couldn't make out what he was saying. I just walked off with my hammer. I hear him yell at Ken to put his pants on. Rob then starts following me to the outside of the club.

"First let me say how sorry I am but I need to know what happened in there." Rob asked.
"Stay back! I have my fucking hammer! I think you know damn well what happened in there!" I replied
"I really don't know anything. I just saw Ken with his pants down and you with a hammer so I honestly can't say I know what was going on."
"Bullshit! You know the man is a slime ball. I am sure I am not the first person he has tried this to."

"Tried what?"

"Dude! The guy has been making awful remarks to me for weeks. He wanted to take advantage of me and I was not gonna let that happen."

Rob was skeptical that his business associate would be such an awful person. I knew I had to get out of there and in turn stay away from there. I thanked Rob for giving me an opportunity but I told him I am not riding home with Ken. Rob offered me a ride but I told him that wasn't an option at this point. So I stormed out of the parking lot with my new hammer and walked. It wasn't a short walk either. I walked all these weird back roads on the off chance Ken would drive by and try to pick me up. I think I made it home around four or five hours later thankfully with no sighting of Ken.

I was just so shaken up by the whole incident that I didn't want to talk to anybody. I had ignored phone calls from friends and family and just sort of secluded myself for the next few weeks. Rob had left me several voicemails, emails, and text messages about wanting me to come back to work. He claimed that Ken was no longer going to be working there, and that Ken wanted to personally apologize to me and that I didn't do any damage to his groin. Not that I cared about that to be honest with you. He asked me if I wanted to press any kind of charges but since I was able to defend myself and get away I figured there would be no point.

I wanted no parts of going back there and I never returned. I wouldn't even go as a patron. The club would eventually close. Ken had given up trying to get with me. Rob still wanted to eventually use me in a video. Kyle had ended up working at another club shortly after the closing. Stefan ended up having more drug issues and having numerous arrests. Travis was the one that I had lost touch with all together. He was trying to call me but I just couldn't bring myself to tell him what happened. I also just didn't want to be associated with him because he was still going to be working at the club. With everything that had happened up to that point I really just wanted to move on with my life.

## CHAPTER 4 – I'm on the highway to hell

A few weeks had passed and I was finally putting all the drama from the night club behind me. I was ready to move on to my next goal. I still wanted to do something with modeling or acting. I had made some connections via social networking and as I had mentioned earlier, one of them was a Gay Porn Producer. There was something alluring about the idea of going into the porn business. I was still eighteen and was quite a few months away from turning nineteen. I had heard a few stories of how people in this type of career path have a short shelf life for their career in entertainment. Once you aren't considered a twink anymore you are practically disposable. So I knew I had to act quickly and at least get a jump start on this potential career path.

I was looking through some messages and this producer had contacted me. At first I just assumed it was some sort of spam message but I was curious and I started to do some of my own research. Everything came back legit and legal so I figured I might as well at least reply and see where this could potentially lead me. This was a while ago so I can't remember much about what the company was called or if they are even still making videos today. We had exchanged a few messages which lead to phone calls, and then finally some face to face camming. Through the webcam he was giving me a tour of his "studio" and I got to meet some of the actors. The models were good looking guys and I was at this point interested in learning more. He wanted to arrange a face to face meeting with me. I told him that I wasn't yet driving at the time. He said he could pay for my flight out to where his studios were located. I had little knowledge of how to even use an airport at this time. I don't know why but I ended up agreeing to do the trip via bus. I would be spending a weekend at this place and the guy would get to know me. I would get to know some of the models and I could do some test videos if I wanted to or potentially even start working if all the paperwork and whatever other requirements they had were processed and on file.

I was going to be taking a bus trip that would take a half a day or longer. I think flying would have been the better option, but at the time I was living with my parents and that was not something I really wanted to discuss. I was already a pretty difficult teenager in my later teenage years. I hated school even though I liked learning. I loved wrestling and basketball and cross country but couldn't do any of those because I just had behaviour issues.  Again I mostly just hung with the wrong crowd of misfits. My parents actually were rather strict in a lot of regards. Nothing that was too severe, but they had their rules and I had to follow them. At one point I just got too cocky and didn't care anymore. I ended up sitting them down and apologizing when I graduated because it was a miracle and that they refused to give up on me. I was no longer that little ungrateful asshole and I was trying to keep the relationship in a positive direction going forward. It was best that I kept this to myself. While I was getting more mature in a lot of ways I was still quite immature when it came to keeping things from my parents. Long story short it was easier for me to walk to the bus station and say that I was going on a weekend trip with, "Nikki"whom they had met once or twice and trusted. Then they wouldn't have to drive me to the airport and ask a million questions.

I really regret taking the bus because everything about the process was such a path of agony toward hell. It was bad enough that I had a five mile walk to the bus station mostly uphill. I got to the bus station and this older woman who had to be about five hundred was helping me. I was listed as the pickup name on the ticket but she evidently kept spelling my name when looking it up and saying I didn't exist. I just figured she was just a miserable old cunt but I was polite to her face because what the hell does being mean accomplish? I mean she was walking proof of that. I couldn't tell if the stink of shit in the air was from her diaper or the broken bathroom.

The bus then gets delayed to make matters worse and my phone was out of service so I couldn't even call to say I might be late. I really should have just walked back home and forgot about the whole thing but I really am one who wants to just continue falling down when shit can't get worse. I figure it could be a learning experience. Eventually the trip finally gets started and the first few hours of my bus ride were surprisingly pleasant. I had actually met a lot of really delightful personalities. One guy was going to visit his girlfriend and was going to propose, another person was going to meet their father for the first time. There was this one woman who was telling me a story of how she had to give up her dreams of being a dancer because of having to take some sort of job to feed her family during the war. I was inspired and knew any struggles I faced would be part of my journey, even though I would never most likely face anything as severe as that.

Since everything was going so well now comes a change over and a new stop. Clearly we stopped in a land of I don't know what the hell to call this place.

You could just feel a new vibe in the atmosphere. Of course I would attract the most eccentric person on the bus. This shorter heavier guy in his twenties sits next to me. He had on cargo shorts and a beat up Grateful Dead shirt on and just smelled of rancid pot. He introduced himself as, Ryan and just started talking to me without me even saying anything to him back. The next two or three hours he just kept on talking and talking. I didn't even once say a word the entire time but just kept staring blankly at him. I honestly thought he was capable of harming me, so I was just being on my guard. I was starting to think of what I had in my bag or on me in case I needed to protect myself. I never wanted to be in any kind of situation like that. He kept talking something about seeing these rabbits. Which I confused for Cedar Rapids and didn't even know the bus was going that way. He then started carrying on about kissing his sister and how her lips tasted as sweet as lemon. The more he was talking the more I was thinking he was as bright as a bat cave. Something wasn't right there and he kept going on. I still never said anything to him. I had no idea why he kept telling me his life story. I knew more about him and his obsession with rabbits and his sister than I cared to ever know. I can probably write a whole book just on them. He talked that way to me until we got to the next station. Which thankfully he got off at. I ended up falling asleep at this point and just waking up as my stop was approaching.

I get to the bus station and there is well dressed thirty something year old guy in some expensive Italian looking suit. I thought there might be some sort of Miami Vice convention in town and that it was a Don Johnson tribute act. This guy actually quite looked like Don Johnson of the 80's. Anyway it wasn't and it turned out the guy was actually looking for me. He saw that I looked confused and asked me if I was meeting Gary. I said "No I am looking for Gary." Since I was an idiot that day. I think he understood that I was tired and just took this long bus ride.

Gary was a nice gentlemen. He was the producer's assistant. I didn't get any odd or uncomfortable type of vibes from him. He just seemed like someone I could chill with on the weekend and have a good time with. I am not sure if that was just a ploy to get me comfortable so I was cautious with how close I would get to this guy. It was a rather short drive to the manor or homestead or whatever the hell you would call a living quarters for a gaggle or gay porn stars. It was late in the evening so I was exhausted but they wanted to rush me in to get started on paperwork. The house was huge and gorgeous of course. Everything just looked like stuff that I'd never be able to afford but maybe I could if I was a rich successful porn star. Something about that was already slightly off putting. It is like they are cock teasing me with money and fancy things which is something I may or may not ever have depending how my career goes. Anyway Gary rushed me to an office and I was told others were around but I didn't see anyone yet. I wasn't sure where they were but here I was being escorted and felt like I wasn't even supposed to be there.

They start going over these forms and checking into my ID and submitting some sort of background checks. I hadn't yet signed anything, but they were making everything sound golden. I got handed this questionnaire about things that I would be comfortable doing on camera or live, would I do multiples, or bareback, and STD status, and would I be willing to get tested regularly. It was all very routine. Then they tell me since I was tired

they wanted me to get some rest but I wasn't
allowed to masturbate or have sexual contact with
any of the other performers that may be staying
there that weekend. They wanted me to get a decent
sized load for my test video. I also wouldn't sign
any of my paperwork till the next day. I was
escorted out of the office and introduced to some of
the other performers. They told me they'd have a
few names selected for me tomorrow and I could
pick one that I liked.

A lot of the performers that were there that
weekend were just out of my league. I felt like a
whale in a sea of twinks. They all had perfect tans,
perfect bodies, perfect skin. I didn't really feel
comfortable with any of them but then this one guy
got my attention.

"You'll be fine. Don't let these guys
intimidate you." I was just at a loss for words
because this guy was giving me attention. He was
your typical blonde haired twink, with a slim body
and blue eyes. He introduced himself (I think it was
Kevin, or Liam, I honestly didn't hear him when he
introduced himself) and we started talking. He
invited me for some tea on the patio.

"Thanks for inviting me out here. I'm a little bit shy around new people." I said

"You got nothing to worry about. You are better looking than a lot of the guys here. You also don't look like a total slut like the actual gay guys here. The straight guys that are here are just assholes."

"Not one you wanna lick either!" I joked.

He actually laughed at my stupid joke and he had such an adorable laugh and a crooked smile that added more charm. I complimented his smile and he seemed shocked.

"Do you really think so? They want me to get my teeth fixed but I am not sure in what way and if that would put me out of action?"

He was still rather new and had only shot a few scenes but felt insecure about his smile. I adored how imperfect it was and thought he would be crazy to fix it. He said it would open up some more opportunities because of how obsessed the industry seems with perfection. I shared some of those insecurities because I never had straight or perfect teeth I never had the desire to get them fixed either. I thought that this might end up causing a similar issue with me.

"It sucks if that's the reason you wouldn't get a lot of work. If it is that important to you than do it otherwise don't compromise your values and be satisfied with less opportunity." I said to him "I really just want to make it and get myself in a better place." He responded.

I wasn't really sure what to say to him at this point because I couldn't relate to wanting something that bad that I would drastically change my appearance. Tanning, and shaving wore about the expectations I was given at this point and that's about the level I was comfortable with. I really wanted to remain as true to myself as I could. I probed him a little further by asking him why he was so dead set on wanting to be successful at all costs. That is when shit really hit the fan and he just started spilling out his life story.

This was a guy who was nineteen. He was already worried that him being nineteen was a disadvantage because some fresh faced eighteen year old could replace him easily. He was telling me from the little experience he had and what he had talked to others about the money wasn't as good as they make it sound, and you have a short shelf life if you don't have a certain look. He felt that he had about a good year or two to really do his best work and then figured the offers would dwindle down because, "that's just how shitty it is."

"I actually hate doing this. I just hate that I am here doing this with my life. I've just fucked up so much at this point and I felt like I had to do this to survive." He cried out.

What do you say to that? I again got awkwardly quiet and was hoping he didn't have a sister that he enjoyed kissing like the weirdo on the bus. I just let him start to cry and tell me about the things he was worried about. He ended up coming closer to me and resting his head on my shoulders. I went into my protective mode and rubbed his back and petted his hair. His words were really resonating with me and I felt like he was someone I had made a connection with. I just felt that he had been seeking someone to just share this with but he didn't trust any of the other performers and seemed like he had nobody in his life that even cared.

"My mother died and shortly after my dad would become abusive and not just in punch me in the face kind of way." He continued to sob.

He began to tell me these tales of how his relationship with his father became so damaged after his mother's death. His father would take out his frustration on him physically, mentally, and sexually. He wanted to really just have a father in his life but not someone he was afraid of. His father would smack him, call him an ungrateful faggot, and make him suck his dick.

"My mother just died only two years ago. A few months went by and then my dad started just taking out aggression. It kept building and getting worse. I turned eighteen and that's when he started getting sexual. The man just stalked me and waited." He cried out to me.

I was feeling heartbroken for the guy and just wanted to cry with him but he needed someone to be strong for him because he was a pure disaster. I let him just continue to talk to me and I offered my support. He was hoping that he could make enough money to get out on his own and not have to worry about being in that situation. He was safely staying with a few friends that he had made and didn't really have a true idea of what home was. He just wanted to make it because for him that would be his chance to become something. He asked me if I could sleep in the same room with him that night because I was the first person that made him feel really comfortable. I had agreed, because I was tired and I just had a lot to think about. He had mentioned about missing opportunity and feeling like he fucked up. These were things that I now had to think about. Is this something that would ruin me or prevent me from one day getting a job? What would happen if I failed and had nowhere to go? He made me think about a lot of things that hadn't really even crossed my mind at this point. I just wanted the weekend to be over.

We went back to the bedroom he was staying in. We both ended up sleeping together in our underwear. There was a certain level of vulnerability that came with that uncharted territory. I felt comfortable enough to sleep like that with him because he let his wall down and I shouldn't need to have a barrier. I cuddled up next to him and spooned him close to me and he whispered out a "Thank You". The skin to skin contact felt more comforting than sensual. I had my own problems and my own issues but nothing that really as major or severe as his. Here we were just two souls that were bonding and becoming one with another. It was quite a powerful thing. It was as if for just a moment we found a safe place. When where no matter what was going on in our individual lives that this was all that mattered.

I still had blended emotions pulsating through my mind in regards to if I even wanted to go through with my audition. I couldn't sleep but he had fallen asleep and I just held him tight. Something about me being with him seemed like if even if we never saw each other again that me being there for him was a sign of hope. I just couldn't come to terms with how he could live his life this way. How was it even possible for him to perform? Did he actually even enjoy it or was it personal hell?

I eventually drifted into a harmonious slumber. We somehow managed to shift positions to the point where we were facing one another while holding onto each other. We went into an abrupt awakening and gazed into each other's eyes with the dim patio lights outside our window illuminating our faces. I was transfixed on his gaze but only because I was trying to dig deeper and read more of his personal story. I don't know if he was receiving some other sort of message but he leaned in closer to my face. We were about to kiss and that is not the silence I was speaking. I tried to pull away but he got closer and our lips locked. I tried to pull away again but he wouldn't let me slip away. We are now passionately kissing each other and he's getting more and more into it with each passing second. I finally get the chance to come up for air and there is a break in our embrace. I use that moment to mention that I have to go to the bathroom. I actually did have to pee but I was holding it for a while because he was so comfortable.

I leave the bed and he doesn't ask me any questions or even imply any sort of disappointment. He was a fantastic kisser but I just wasn't ready for anything at that point. I wasn't sure if he would want it to turn into some sort of relationship or if it would just be a fling but I wasn't ready to find out. Plus with him dealing with all those issues, I didn't want to be the one to trigger some sort of mental breakdown. I took a few minutes longer in the bathroom to process my thoughts. I liked this guy as a friend but I didn't want a relationship and I sure in hell didn't want a hook up. When I returned back to the bed he was back asleep. I would fall back asleep next to him with a lot more on my mind.

When we woke up he didn't mention kissing me or anything happening last night. He asked me how I slept and if he snored or talked in his sleep. I don't know if he wasn't aware what happened or if he was just pretending he didn't. I had told him of my decision and now it was time to tell the boss man the same thing. I had decided that this wasn't something I was ready to do. I was turning down the offer. He had wanted to exchange contact information to keep in touch. He would go on to tell me about how last night meant so much to him and that nobody else in his life ever took that much of an interest. He wanted to keep in touch because for the first time he felt he had a real friend in his life. I was thrilled that we would remain friends and I could see him flourish in his career or whatever happens in his life.

Going into the producer's office was overwhelming. I was nervous about the conversation but I was confident that I made the right choice. They still wanted to work with me and were a bit too pushy for my liking. They discussed how they could pay me more and made me "promises". There was something unsettling about that. Now they are offering me more? Why should I have settled for less in the first place? I had declined anything they threw at me no matter how tempting they made it sound. My mind was made up and I didn't want to be taken advantage of which is how any of their offers were making me feel. I got my stuff together and ended up leaving early and headed back for the bus ride home. On the way home I would exchange a few messages with my new friend.

We actually kept in contact for quite a while after the whole ordeal. Much longer than I thought was even possible in the first place. He had shot a few more scenes but an HIV scare would deter him away from continuing to do anymore work with the company. I wasn't sure to what extent he meant that. Did one of the other performers contact it or was he worried he might have performed with someone who did? He narrowly avoided getting into drugs because he had a cousin intervene, but again I know little about what happened. He was a good friend for a while but after a few visits and our lives taking different paths we lost touch as people do. The last I heard he had begun dating someone and this person was a really good influence on his life. He moved in with that person after dating for a few months and I am not sure what happened after that. I'm glad he found happiness because he honestly deserved it and I just hope it lasted for him.

## CHAPTER 5 – Falling in love with wrestling

I'm going to back track slightly for a bit because I feel the first few chapters were heavy hitting and there was already a lot of drama and obstacles to overcome. I want to discuss something more positive. This actually doesn't really stray too far from the timeline as far as sequence goes. We can take a detour and just go back a few years prior. We are going back in time to my high school days. It will give you some more back story because we could always use more of that. Wrestling was something that I was always passionate about. I would meet up for frequent matches with my best friend, Will. I had briefly discussed him earlier in the book when I was talking about a cheating bitch. He and I grew up together and I would meet up with him for pro style matches. We had a good chemistry that is often hard to replicate. Wrestling with him made me develop my passion even more and encouraged me to start thinking of how to get to the next level.

Growing up we would attend local pro wrestling shows. We were teenagers and had an interest in learning more about pro wrestling but weren't sure if our parents would be on board with the idea. At the time one of the promotions was sort

of a big deal. It was ran by one of the legendary
Wild Samoans. Anyone who knows anything about
pro wrestling will know their names. They always
put on incredible shows and had incredible talent.
We wanted to be a part of that someday. We used to
stay after the shows and hang around and get to
know some of the wrestlers and the wrestler's
families. We would also help fold up chairs, clean,
and help the wrestlers get out of there faster. We
had ended up meeting up with a guy who was
around our age at the time. He hold told us that his
dad was a wrestler and would occasionally wrestle
on some of the other shows by some other
promotions. We would slowly become friends with
him after attending a few of the local wrestling
shows. He then invited us to attend his dad's
training facility to watch some of the training to see
if it was something we would be interested in. His
dad wasn't affiliated with the Wild Samoans or even
actively wrestling for their promotion. He had
claimed that he had trained with them at one point
and attended seminars that they held to fine tune his
skills. I didn't really care about any of that but it
sounded good enough to me.

We went to the training school and we
watched the students learning basics, doing bumps,

running ropes, doing rolls, drills and everything else that gets your body conditioned to go in the ring for as long as you have to. It was exciting to watch and it was something that I really wanted to get my feet wet with. I couldn't afford to enroll in the school, but we were asked if we would be interested in doing a try out to see if it was something we were interested in. Somehow we convinced our parents to let us do it. I think they were just happy we found an activity that was keeping us at of trouble and thought it was school related. The try out would be a lot of the stuff that we were watching. Taking basic bumps, seeing how well we listened to instruction, some basic drills. We agreed to do the tryout and set it up for one of the following nights.

I remember being so focused and trying hard not to think about what I was doing. The more you think the more chance you mess up. I remember also trying to outdo Will because even though I was in better shape he was slightly more athletic than me. So that right there was already a lot to compete with. I remember his dad showing us about tucking our chin and the slow start of falling backwards from a squatted position. I was instantly a natural at taking bumps. I just didn't know enough about selling and reacting to make it look more convincing. Those are things that I would learn later on. Doing face bumps and flip bumps were a little intimidating at first. Falling from my knees face first not knowing if I would break my nose was not exactly fun. I got accustomed to it. Before we could even do the flip bumps we would have to practice hooking and throwing ourselves over each other. One person would get on hands and knees and the other would hook on flip over to get use to using your own momentum to throw yourself over. It also helped with the feeling of getting used to being flipped. Turned out to be a pretty standard way of doing things and I'd use a lot of the same techniques.

Doing front, side, and back rolls was rather easy for me. I think running the ropes was probably the hardest for me. I wasn't yet very tall and hitting the ropes took a little getting used to. It is a hard feeling to really describe for the first time. While they have some give to them you are basically trying to attack them and they are leaving welts in your back at the same time. Not exactly the most pleasant feeling the first time you do it.

I was hooked from the tryout but I wasn't going to be able to continue training without any money. We were both in that same situation. We were interested but would mostly be at the point where we would hang around and hope we could get some ring time. They knew as much as we liked to help out at other shows. They would let us work a few of the shows and learn about paying our dues in exchange for some extra training until we could start making payments somehow. We started cutting grass, cleaning pools, selling old toys, and doing whatever odd chores we could for people to raise some money. We would pay as we go and when we could and start to learn a lot of moves and more about the wrestling business in general. We were starting to make some progress and while it would be a while until we were match ready, mostly because we were too young to be booked on many shows aside from any this guy's dad would do. We started just practicing on our own time in a field near where we lived. We would make wrestling mats out of old plywood and carpet or whatever we had laying around and start practicing. We worked on our move sets and our performance. I might also add we had some stellar matches for two guys who were just practicing. One was a three hour match with a lot of back and forth and a wide variety of chain moves.

Just as things were going from one positive to another things took a turn for the worse and shit hit the fan. Will had broken his arm from a non-wrestling related injury. I think he was trying out for something at school but took a fall hard. The guy who was running the training school had a heart attack. That took him out of action and he was no longer able to be physical. His son wasn't able to run the school by himself and some of the other trainers just quit in his absence. While he recovered from the heart attack there was no training going on. The school would close down for a while and that meant we were shit out of luck. I couldn't afford training anywhere else and had just been working on a handshake type of deal.

Will, would slowly lose interest in wrestling and then I was stuck by myself with no other options. Will and I would still have some matches after his arm healed but I could tell that he wasn't enjoying it as much. He had lost his passion and it was so one sided that It was even becoming less enjoyable for me. I knew I didn't want to give up but I also had to be realistic. Wrestling him had really helped me turn into a decent wrestler. I just wasn't going to be able to continue to train. We had went to this one show and one of the promotions was leaving town but having a big show. One of the wrestlers I admired watching, Luna Vachon, was making an appearance.

We went to the show and we watched her "bit" in the show. I had ran into her while I was going on my way to the bathroom. I introduced myself and shook her hand and told her she did a fantastic job. She posed for a picture with me and made sure I was satisfied with the photo before I left. I then mentioned that I was training but my trainer had a setback and I couldn't train and I was feeling discouraged.

She told me, "There was a path that we were given and that if you have the talent and drive you could follow the path the way it was meant to be followed." I wasn't really sure what that meant exactly but I thanked her for her time and let her get on her way. It was just nice to hear some words of encouragement from someone that I admired.

I didn't quite know what the next step to take was. I knew that I wanted to do wrestling in some regard. The only other opportunity I had was joining my high school wrestling team. Even though that was way different from what I was used to it was something I wanted to improve at since I hadn't had much experience in that area. Wrestling across the spectrum was a natural fit for me. I think there was a three day try out and conditioning that was coming up. I made friends with someone who was on the team and I was determined to make the team. I believe his name was, Adam. I don't even remember how I got the courage to approach him and ask him to help me out but I did. I had walked up and introduced myself and asked him if he was looking for someone to practice with. Turns out he was always looking to practice so I had an in. We'd arranged to meet up after school and get in some practice. I didn't have much experience but he was willing to coach me. He taught me a few holds and reversals and just took me under his wing. He really wanted to improve himself and be one of the best on the team. We were also in the same weight class so we were a natural fit for one another. While he was teaching me he was pushing me to go hard so I could actually give him a challenge. I had a natural quickness to me both in terms of ability and learning. It was the same situation when I played basketball. I wasn't the tallest player but I was quick and could maneuver in and out of tight spaces with ease. That was something that came in hand when it came to doing more amateur type of wrestling. So while I was improving and learning he was also using me to get himself to be much better. I didn't care because it was helping me out and I needed the help.

The problem was sometime between practicing with him and the actual conditioning and tryouts that I lost sight of my goal. While I was always athletic to an extent, I felt I never fit in with the jocks or the popular crew. That just was never my type of thing. I had a lot more in common with the people of drama club and the band geeks. Status was a big thing and I felt a lot of pressure to have a group that accepted me. Every group of course has those few sour apples and I of course fell in with them. I don't know why I tried so hard to impress these people when they were going to end up accomplishing nothing with their lives. There was a certain thrill to skipping school and going on random day trips to go shopping or go to the beach. It is when I started hanging out with this troublesome crowd and my attitude shifted. I felt that I had finally meshed with what I thought was a cool crowd. Close friends and family were noticing the changes in me but I just didn't care. I started to skip school more and when I was there I was either a bully for no reason, or narrowly avoiding getting into a fight.

I started to spend a lot of time in the in school suspension and detention. As weird as it sounds I even started to find more in common with a lot of the people that were also there. A lot of us felt like we were outcasts and had our own personal issues. Some of them had severe anxiety, depression or just bad social or home lives. I had a good life at home but could relate to not feeling like you belong. It also got me a chance to actually do homework and focus on school work because there wasn't issues with overcrowded class rooms. So I eventually just started to act out even more just so I could get into trouble. I'd talk back to teachers, give almost anyone an attitude, and just be a real jerk because I could. There was an after school boot camp program that I was headed for. That was near military like with strict drills, obstacle courses, and structure. That actually sounded like more of a reward because it was something I wasn't getting in school. I think I did something where I threw my food at someone and dumped milk on them and I was put on two weeks of after school cleaning duty with the cleaning ladies. I guess that was supposed to be punishment.

I actually really enjoyed helping them out because they were all very interesting women. I also felt like I had a purpose. Here I was doing something good and working my ass off. It was that same feeling I got when I was training for wrestling. I felt like I was accomplishing something.

I remember one of the ladies was talking to me one day when we were on a lunch break with one of the snacks she would sneak for me. She started asking me about my life and what my hobbies were. She took an interest in my life and that struck a positive chord with me. I told her about how I wanted to do more with wrestling both professionally and on the wrestling team. She saw a ton of potential in me and knew I was a decent person deep inside. It was another case of I feel like someone is accepting me and I'm going to open up to them because I often struggled with feeling accepted. Soon enough my assignment would come to an end and I was filled some motivation to start getting the things I wanted.

Sadly I couldn't be a part of the wrestling team because my grades were starting to slip, and with me being in detention and suspension as often as I was I would not be able to participate. I blew my chances and it stung a bit. I was bitter but I only had myself to blame. Adam started to socialize with me less because I wasn't on the team but he was still

wanting to get some practice in. It was more of I was
the last option available to him so if his other
options fell through at least he could use me.

I got to a point where I realized that I needed
to graduate so I had to pull everything together. At
some point I actually started just showing up and
staying. People were starting to notice that I had less
of an attitude and more of a drive. I was in a speech
& drama class and I had two really good friends that
were keeping me in line. I stopped hanging out with
the more troublesome students and started finding
some more positive influences. Whatever the hell I
did managed to somehow work. I was able to turn
my grades around and bring myself up from near
failure and having to repeat a grade. I think that was
also one of the hidden motivators. Just already being
there and not wanting to be there and realizing that
I'd never have to come back was a good thing. Part
of me wanted to fail so I could have another try at
the wrestling team but I was also getting to the point
where I think it was time to move on from that. If
wrestling was something that I was meant to do
then I'd find a way to do it after high school. In
some ways I felt that wrestling was consuming my
life. I had been following it my entire life and had
been addicted to my local indy scene and just

wanted to be a part of it. I started to think that it was best to put any of my wrestling hopes on hold. It came time for graduation and now I had to figure out what the hell I wanted to do with my life. I knew that college wasn't for me so I just started looking for work. I figured I could work like a normal person while ultimately still doing something in the entertainment world on the side. I knew I was in for one hell of a ride whatever would come next.

# CHAPTER 6 – You better work

I mentioned earlier in the book about my experience working in the gay club. That happened right after my eighteenth birthday. Then shortly after that was the whole fiasco with the whole almost getting involved in adult entertainment industry. I still wanted to do something in the entertainment world but not something that I was going to be taking my clothes off. I just didn't know what. I also knew that I wanted my life to calm down because I craved normalcy at that point. I took an overnight job stocking shelves and on weekends I was pet groomer. It was one of the family businesses so I helped out on occasion. I've always enjoyed working with animals. In my earlier years of high school, I volunteered at several of the no kill shelters. Pet grooming was something else I was passionate about but not something I wanted to be doing for the rest of my life.

My days would consist of going to pet expos to cheer on colleagues who would enter grooming competitions. Then try to score free products for the salon. As well as traveling to attend casting calls, or auditions. After all I still wanted to do something in the entertainment world.

As much as I wanted to live a normal life I still wanted to just entertain people. I got involved with a few of the local theatre groups but early on would only get small parts that really had no lines. I stuck with that for a few months and managed to snag a part in, "Bell, Book, and Candle." I auditioned for Nicky who in the film version was played by, Jack Lemmon. I was thrilled to finally have some lines. It was one of my favorite classic movies. It was ridiculous but one of those ridiculous and still cheesy good movies, at least I thought so. Remembering lines was a bit harder than I thought it would be.

I just remember rehearsing with anyone who would let me get the practice. I was a nervous wreck up until opening night. That week the final rehearsals I thought for sure I would mess something up. I had one hell of a front put up. On the outside I was calm and cool but the inside was the total opposite. Something changed once I walked onto stage. The audience was difficult to see because of the bright lights aimed towards the stage. I had friends and family in the crowd that was there to cheer me on but I could barely make out their faces. Thinking I would vomit I was surprised when I actually felt a spark. I had this energy inside of me and this confidence that I lacked prior. I was completely comfortable and I had no idea why. I had this charisma, this stage presences, and could actually act. I loved the feeling and I knew that it was something that I had to continue to do. I wanted to look into more acting opportunity. These are all things that would help me later in my wrestling career. I started to just go after any opportunity that would come my way.

I went to a few of the local colleges that had film programs. One because I was actually interested in doing video editing, and production. So I wanted to learn more about their programs. The other was to see if I could find student films to try out for. I would just go to the campus and walk around and find their main hall or building where the students would hang out. I'd look at any and all bulletin board postings to see if there were upcoming auditions for anything. I wasn't sure if I would have to be a student, but I was sure I could figure out something to pretend I was. I mean I was trying to get more acting experience after all. I would send emails, texts, phone calls or show up at posted audition times depending what the flyer asked in hopes of getting some work. I knew these wouldn't be paid projects but as with in wrestling it is more of a pay your dues kind of thing and work your way up the ladder. I had to start somewhere.

I managed to get myself a few auditions but I wasn't getting selected and there were people that were just better than me. I started to get rejection after rejection but I kept pushing through because I knew I'd eventually get a part. Either I would be the perfect fit or there would be nobody else for the role.

I ended up getting selected for some really low budget horror type of student film. It was also the first time that I got a main role which in this case was the lead survivor. I think it was maybe forty minutes running time. It had a rather ridiculous plot. There was something about the campus being haunted. It was filmed in various dorm rooms, the woods around school, and nearby abandoned houses. That was one of the places my character had to search for clues to try to figure out what was going on. I had an on screen girlfriend and we had to do a couple of love scenes. That was odd for me to take part in. I hadn't had much experience with women and being sensual with them. Here she was also a few years older than I was. I think she was twenty-three and here I was still eighteen. She was very pretty of course with her straight blonde hair, and her slim figure. One of our scenes involved getting down to our underwear and making out. Another one involved me having to save her from the spirit creature in a swimming pool.

I enjoyed the process and I actually liked acting. I have no idea if the movie ever got finished. I only ever saw a trailer at screening for an upcoming student film festival. I don't know if it was finished in time. I didn't get a chance to attend the festival and I never heard from any of the people involved with the filming. It wouldn't be the last time that a project I got involved with would never see the light of day. I wasn't even aware that was a thing. Like how could you put that much work into something and then never finish it? I didn't realize things like money and deadlines were an issue.

I liked acting but I also wanted to do more. Even to this day I get bored with routine and like to change things up once in a while. I find new hobbies all the time and some of them stick and others are just a fad. That seemed to also be true for different parts of my entertainment career. I really wanted to get involved with modeling. I also thought getting an agent or working with a modeling agency could help my acting career. So of course I looked into what my options were as far as modeling went.

I don't know if it was timing or just because it was meant to be but one day on break at work I was flipping through the classified ads in the newspaper. I see in bold lettering that this modeling agency is holding a casting call looking for new talent. There were dates of when the seminar would be held and what you should bring. I figured this was a good opportunity that I shouldn't pass up.

This seminar and casting thing was held at some sort of banquet hall. There were easily hundreds of people that showed up to this thing. I had purchased a new outfit just for the casting. I was wearing these ripped jeans (that was legit a fashion thing at the time, purchasing jeans with pre made holes in them) and I wore a this neon green button down short sleeve shirt with a grey light thermal underneath. Layering clothes was just in at the time. I got my hair cut with this choppy, and messy layered tussled look. I added some color so it was brown with some reddish brown low lights. I looked and felt amazing but I also didn't want to seem like I was over doing it, like many others who showed up were. There were girls with orange tans and fried highlighted hair, and white out bleached teeth. They would literally glow under a black light if one was there.

I was sitting in the crowd and the casting agent woman came out to a chorus of clicking high heels. She was dressed sharply in a slim fitting black pant suit. Her highlighted hair was flat ironed and her make up slightly overdone and slightly off tone. She had a fair complexion but her face was slightly darker from the make up. She had on this bright pink lipstick. She was pretty but I felt like she was trying too hard to make an impression.

She started talking about the company and her experience in the industry. She was talking about how you would have to be prepared to miss work for an audition or a casting. Have to be available at a moment's notice. If you weren't ready for that kind of lifestyle to leave the room now. A few people got up on that spot and walked out. She would go on to insult them, saying how they had no passion and would never survive the industry. The next part came these video interviews with a various panel. They wanted you to do a few poses to see how well you could handle direction as well as get a sense of your personality. I sort of blanked out on my interview and really just had no idea what it was that I even wanted to say. I started talking about how I wanted to visit Ireland and that was about all

I could muster up. I thought for sure I had blown my audition. I left feeling defeated.

The next day I had received a phone call stating that they were interested in me. I was a bit excited but I was also very cautious. Turns out that they were doing a photoshoot for the people they chose at the same place. This was the catch though. You would have to use their photographer and pay for your own pictures before signing. That seemed strange to me. I had the money ready and it was only around $250 but something didn't seem right with that idea. It seemed like it was just as crowded as it was a few days prior. There was no way that they could pick each one of these people. Basically, you pay their fee and you may or may not get work. There are a ton of agencies that operate that way and technically it isn't a scam because you aren't guaranteed work and you are put in their system with the chance you may get work.  So they aren't just taking your money and running. Some people get booked. A small number of people manage to get work that way but that is not the best way to find work at all. I shouldn't have to be shelling out money for you to find me work.

I politely told them that I changed my mind and right now was not a good time for me. I didn't honestly know what I wanted my next move to be. I tried my hand at a few different things with no luck. I frequently went to casting calls in New York in hopes of getting on a game show or a reality show. I wasn't having any luck with that and I didn't want to keep missing work to go to auditions because I wanted to focus on getting to travel a bit. I was determined to get to Ireland or The U.K. because there was a lot of Irish and English in my ancestry and I wanted to explore that a bit more. That would come in due time. I took a break from trying to become famous and focused on working to save money and then just some bad dating.

# <u>CHAPTER 7 – I want a boyfriend</u>

I had focused so much of my time on wrestling, doing the local theatre, auditions, and trying to become famous that I never took the time to date anyone. I was so focused on myself. I thought maybe it is time I start dating. That turned out to be quite a mistake. I ended up dating a circus of clowns.

I was staying with my cousin for a bit of time. She was a few years older than I was and more of a big sister. I never really felt like I had and older brother or sister that I could actually look up to. In a lot of ways she filled in that gap. I could share things with her that I couldn't share with other people. So it made bringing home dates easier and she had good perception and could tell me when I was making a bad choice. The problem was I didn't want to listen and I just had to make my own mistakes.

One of the first guys that peaked my interest was some guy who called himself Spike. He was just a few years older than I. I think his real name was Arthur and he just didn't like his name. I think he was trying to mold himself after Spike from Buffy the Vampire Slayer. Only he was twenty times stranger. We hung out a few times. Mostly just rented movies from the video store and had pizza. He had two sides to him. He had this sweet and sincere side. Then he also had this side where he would go into this demonic freak which he would usually unleash when we were in public. It was hard to describe exactly what he would do. He was verbally abusive to a lot of people around him. He would insult people for no reason and almost get into fights. He told me that he felt comfortable with me. I was fascinated by the sweet side but scared to death of the wild side.

I walked over to his place one day and he told me he wanted me to meet his parents. Little did I know that he was actually going to choose that moment to "come out" to them and tell them that I was his "boyfriend". It was one of the strangest moments of my life. I had never been in this situation. I never really came out to anyone aside from my cousin and that was just because she asked me. Him and I sat on one couch and his parents sat on another couch across the room. The room was small but it felt as if there were multiple football fields between us. He would then make his announcement and of course we were hoping for the touchdown celebration. Hearing him say that he was gay and this is my boyfriend (which I didn't even know we were more than a casual thing.) was hard to process for me. It was even harder for his parents and this is where it got awkward.

They start asking me all sorts of questions. They want to know where I'm from, who I've blown and everything in between. I remember his best friend Lindsay, giving us a blessing and her approving of me. That was once a thing where you had to meet the best friend and they had to approve. I just don't think I was winning over his parents. His mother was the one that kept asking all the heavy hitting questions. She started asking about safe sex and we weren't even having sex. His father on the other hand looked flushed with disappointment. I was at the point where I was uncomfortable to be there because now how would they handle me? What would happen to him?

I told his parents that it was a pleasure to meet them and then I left for the night. A few nights later we would go on what would be one of our final dates. He was driving me around town and he found a parking lot and he pulled over we just sat in this mostly empty parking lot. There were only a few cars there that were parked overnight. He rests his hand on my lap and starts to feel my leg up and down. He leans in and kisses me and I am holding back. I just don't feel comfortable in this parking lot. I stop him and ask him if he heard something outside. He assures me that it is just my mind playing tricks on me. I insist that I hear some yelling and that we should leave the parking lot. Him feeling defeated grabs a flashlight from the glove box and tells me to wait here while he goes outside to look.

He comes running back to the car because there is a person laying under one of the cars in the parking lot. Now I am thinking the absolute worst case scenario here. Was this guy beat up and he was the one screaming? Was someone screaming because they just saw him there looking lifeless? He tells me he thinks the guy might be dead. He gets on the phone and calls emergency services. I tell him to lock the doors because we clearly aren't somewhere safe. He decides to get out of the car to go check on this person. I am pleading with him not to go because what happens if someone comes back to jump him or something? He checks on the guy and he doesn't see any signs of breathing. They say that they are going to send someone. As he is walking back to the car. The guy that was laying unconscious suddenly gets up and has a bottle in his hand. I am thinking oh my god he is going to attack him. The guy turns to Spike and says "What the fuck man I am trying to take a nap here! I am going somewhere else and don't follow me!" This guy gets up and just walks away. We tell emergency services what happened and they said they would send someone to the area but he just sounds like the one homeless drunk that hangs around that area. We ask if we need to stay till they got there but they tell us we are fine to leave because the guy was most likely fine, and would only bother us more if we stayed.

I was just in shock with everything that had happened that week. I told Spike that I only wanted to be friends. That was pretty much the last time that I would talk to him. He was too unpredictable and I felt unsafe with him. The drunk guy laying under a car late at night and coming after us was just the final straw. On an unrelated note it was not the last time I saw the drunk guy. I went shopping in a nearby plaza a few weeks later and there he was just sitting outside and drinking a beer and begging for change. I approached and gave him a five-dollar bill and hoping he went and got a cheap lunch with it. The scary thing is I felt more comfortable approaching him compared to approaching Spike after that night.

The next guy that I ended up with almost made Spike look normal. He pretty much looked like a carbon copy of Napoleon Dynamite. Had the same monotone voice and flat personality. He was about a year older than I was. We met through a mutual friend and that was a disaster from the start. I really don't know what I saw in him. I think if anything it was more of a physical relationship. He was a really good kisser and he wasn't all that good looking. He was also good at sucking dick which is probably really the only reason I hung out with him as much as I did. I was just horny all the time as any eighteen or nineteen year old male would normally be.

I had him meet a few of my friends and he rubbed them all the wrong way instantly. One of my friends said I better guard my valuables because he looks like he would steal everything I own. Another one of my friends said there were slight clues and vibes coming off that make him seem mentally unstable to some degree and he could potentially be abusive. He met my aunt and he met my grandmother and neither one of them was to impressed by him. They wouldn't tell me to my face that he was no good but they dropped enough hints that I was starting to pick up on. It wasn't that I was

too blind to see all of this, I just was happy that I
was getting some action.

We had this thing where I would go back to
his apartment after hunting for vacuum cleaners. He
had this hobby of finding vacuums in the trash and
repairing them in hopes to turn a profit. He didn't
have a real job and that is mostly what he did. It was
just one of his many odd quirks. Anyway usually we
would go back to his apartment or he would tell me
to come over at certain times. Mostly so we could
fool around or I could watch him repair a vacuum. I
was working at my job  a lot of the time so I was
oblivious to his choosy times. Turned out there was
a reason for why he only wanted to hang out at
certain times and I was about to find out why.

He left me a voicemail telling me to come
over at this one time. Only I was working overtime
that week and I had my days mixed up so I turned
up on the wrong day and the wrong time. I showed
up to his apartment and the door was unlocked.
Normally everything was locked because he didn't
have the most trustworthy neighbors. I let myself in
and had my cell phone ready in case there was some
sort of emergency. The apartment was quiet and
there were no signs of an intruder or no mess that
would of indicated someone was there. I went into

the bedroom and thought I would wait there because maybe he had ran to the store or was out for a walk and just forgot to lock the door.

His room smelled of some generic wood forest scented type of cologne. I thought it was odd because he didn't wear cologne. I went to go make a phone call and I had dropped my phone. When I went to pick up my phone I found a a crumbled up piece of paper on the floor. This was odd because one of his other quirks was being a huge neat freak. So paper on the ground was not something that normally flied. I crumbled the paper and it was some sort of note. The note was about someone who wanted to meet him for sex in another apartment. Him and I weren't having sex aside from oral or getting each other off.

I am not sure why he threw the note on the floor but I was pissed off that he had been lying to me about seeing other people. No wonder most of my friends and family didn't like him. They detected that he was a scum and I was just blinded by lust. I decided I was going to go over to the apartment number and raise some hell.

I marched over to the apartment that was listed on the note and banged on the door. Nobody was answering. The neighbor came out to see why I was banging on the door so loudly and it turned out that she knew me and knew that I was hanging around Napoleon. I didn't know much about her aside from that she was about twenty-five and liked her cigarettes and booze. He was She invited me in and things just got more awkward from here.

I was asking if they had seen him and they didn't know where he was. Then they were drinking and smoking and just having casual conversation with me. They were acting like we were some sort of best friends and I should enjoy chilling with them. Since I had nothing else to do I stayed for a bit to see if I could get some more information from them. Only instead of giving me information they started to come onto me. Her and her boyfriend cornered me on their couch and each put one of their hands on my leg and tried to nibble on my ear. I got up from the couch and they then asked me if a drink would loosen me up and make me more comfortable. I decided to get up and leave and I have no idea if they even cared at that point. They started to make out with each other and I just went back over to Napoleon's apartment. I actually had left a book over there that I was reading and wanted to pick it up on my way home because I had to return it to the library. So I needed to get it before I completely forgot about it.

I get back to his apartment and walk in and he is being fucked by some random black guy who looks to be about forty years old. My face lost all expression and I just grabbed my book and didn't say a word. They both looked at me and they didn't even look phased by me. There was no surprise and no shock. The black guy asked me if I cared to join but I completely pretended that I didn't hear what he said. I walked out and put my earphones in and played music on my mp3 player and walked home and tried to forget about the whole thing.

When I got home I had several messages from Napoleon on my computer. I had left my messenger program open with an away message up most of the time. There were several messages telling me that iw wasn't what it looked like. How could it not be what it looked like? It looked like you were getting fucked by a black man with a giant dick! Then he was mad at me for going over to his friend's house behind his back. So he was having sex with another person after telling me for weeks that I was the only person he was seeing. Yet I am the bad guy because I went over his friend's apartment?

It didn't take long for me to move on. The next guy I got involved with was probably one of my biggest mistakes but I was starting to learn and was getting much more perceptive. This guy's name was Christian but hated that name so I had to call him Chris. Nikki, one of the best friends that I wrote about earlier wanted to take a bus trip to one of the big shopping malls when that was actually a thing. The mall was about two hours away from where I was living at the time. Nikki and I would take several bus trips sometimes that were weekend long events or just day trips. While shopping at the mall we ended up going into one of those preppy and snobby clothing stores. The ones where they play the loud music, you can't see where you are going and all the models on the advertisements are beyond photoshopped. I notice this guy when I walk in and I was drawn to him. He was slim, had a short Cesar type of haircut, incredible deep colbalt blue eyes. He was practically a walking billboard for the store, tight ripped jeans, tight collared shirt, and fancy scarf. I looked nothing like that and nothing in this store was something that I would normally wear. I really only liked the socks and underwear. When we walk in he comes over to ask us if we needed any help. I instantly say no because it is just a pre programmed response. He walks away but casually folds clothes nearby us and sort of follows us around the store. At this point I just think he is trying to make sure we don't steal. Nikki is convinced that he is actually interested in me. He comes back over and asks us again if we needed help. This time I tell him if there was a guy I wanted to go on a date and wanted to look really cute what should I get from this store? It was a horrible question and I thought for sure he would think I was an idiot. He actually laughed and then showed me a few different things. Nikki was asking probing questions to learn more about him and we actually had some things in common. I ended up trying something on that I really liked but I actually couldn't afford to buy it that week. Chris really liked the way the outfit looked on me. He told me he thought I looked adorable in it. I didn't know if it was his inner sales man or if he really thought I looked good. I don't know what came over me but instead of giving him a thank you. I asked him if he would go on a date with me if I wore this outfit. The question made no sense and I was so embarrassed but he quickly replied with a "yes" and a "when".

It didn't occur to me that I actually lived almost two hours away. I wasn't sure how any of this was going to work but I had a date lined up.

The first date wasn't anything spectacular. I believe we just did the typical dinner and a movie type of thing. We hit it off pretty well and I wanted to see more of him. I told him that I didn't live very close. He was willing to come up and see me a few times. He asked if I would be ok doing a long distance type of thing if it came to that. I was falling fast for him and wanted it to work so I instantly said yes. Little did I know that there was a reason he wanted a long distance relationship but I'll get to that.

We worked it out to where I would spend my weekends over at his place. We ended up dating for a few months. Things were going so well. Our relationship was starting to get a bit stronger. We were starting to open up more to each other, it went from more casual to more romantic. We got to the point where we made the relationship official and agreed to only see each other.

His best friend. I can't remember her name I want to call her Shelly even though that is not even close. She was kind of a slob and a moocher. She had this wonderful idea about the three of us moving in together and finding a place together. I would only be able to spend the weekends there for the next month or two until I could transfer down that way but I considered the idea.

Shelly was friends with this older woman. She had to be somewhere over seventy. There was an apartment for rent above her and she was able to get a discount on the rent. This woman was strange as all hell. Her name was Judith and when I met her she asked me if I had any pimples on my body that I wanted her to pop. Shelly and Chris loved the apartment. I thought it was kind of lacking but I wanted to get more serious about Chris. I told them that I wouldn't be able to sign a lease right away with me still not being in the area. They got the apartment and I gave my third of the first month's rent. I ended up calling off of work for a few days just so I can spend more time with Chris. His twenty-third birthday was coming up and I wanted to be there with him for his birthday. I think I was starting to spend too much time with him.

Things started to change once we were in that apartment and he was no longer living with his mother. He started to get a bit more distant and then I was finding out secret after secret. He woke up right before me one morning and he didn't know I was awake. He was throwing up in the bathroom. When he got back to the room I asked him if he was alright and he brushed it off. I thought that was kind of strange. Later that night we had food delivered and he barely ate anything. Then he went back to the bathroom but this time he turned the radio on to drown out the sounds of vomit. I went outside the door and listened to him throw up, and it didn't sound natural. It sounded like he was forcing himself to throw up. I would later discover that he was battling bulimia and this was something he was very embarrassed about. Shelly was the one who let it slip by complete accident. She was talking to me one night like I actually was already aware. He never told me and that was something I wasn't very happy about.

I felt like I had been lied to or that I wasn't good enough to reach out to. It hurt and I started to get a bit distant. I started picking up extra hours at work so I would have an excuse to avoid going over there. Part of me wanted to date him still but the other part knew something didn't feel right. Next month's rent was coming up and I was holding off on giving my portion. I wasn't on the lease so I was under no obligation to actually pay any rent. Chris and Shelly kept asking about it and I just made up some bullshit excuse on how there was mistake on my check so they held it till the next pay period. I would spend one more weekend in that apartment and this would be the final straw. He was sleeping and I was getting random text messages. First thinking it was some sort of joke, I laughed it off and ignored it. Then they kept on texting me and the texts were getting dirtier and dirtier. Little did I know that the messages were meant for Chris and he gave this guy my number by accident. The guy went into heavy detail on their encounters. I didn't have to ask any questions. He just kept feeding me more and more information. Part of me felt like it was just some guy that wanted to get with him so was making shit up to make me dump him. The other part of me, actually believed this.

I stopped responding to the text messages and woke up Chris to tell him that I was leaving earlier than anticipated. I was going to pick up more hours at work that week and really could use the money. I mean it wasn't a total lie! I get back to work the next night and then the following morning met Nikki for breakfast. I needed someone to talk, and I wanted to break things off with Chris. I just wasn't sure how to go about it.

In the middle of breakfast Chris calls me and before I can even say anything he just starts sobbing, "I'm so sorry, I feel like a horrible person. I had sex with my ex after you left last night." I just hung up the phone. It didn't bother me that he was having sex with another person. I wasn't a very sexual person so I had to get to know a person or feel a deep connection with them before I would go all the way. I was overworked, stressed, and really tired. I just didn't want to have that kind of conversation. I also tried to hold my head up and stay strong. I was acting as if it didn't bother me but it did. It was a crushing defeat.

He continued to call over the next few weeks. He needed money, he needed food, and he wanted me get him these things. Initially it was hard to say no, but once I stuck to it I was glad I did. I said to him, "I'm sorry but you are just gonna have to get some Ramen Noodles and manage." Once he realized I wouldn't let him mooch money off me, he stopped talking to me really fast. I was proud of myself though. My intuition was telling me something was off and I followed it. I was learning more about  how despicable some people could be. These were important lessons for me.

At one point I decided to start releasing my own videos that were set up similar to a reality show. I was just releasing mini ten to fifteen minute episodes of just some of my recent adventures with friends and family, that I edited together. Either myself or one of my friends would record whatever adventure we were on. Honestly it was pretty pointless and terrible looking back at it. Things like following my friends and me playing a prank on another friend, going on a day trip and interacting with a strange person on the bus. Later on some more drama would start happening and then I was looking for those opportunities to record in hopes of getting views. I'll get more into that in a later chapter, but this next guy sort of ties into that and the wild dating circle.

For the show this one friend and I were going on a day trip to some random city. She and I would just record us getting lost navigating a big city in hopes that it was entertaining. Sadly it wasn't! I ended up planning a last minute date with some guy that I had been texting that happened to live in that city. We thought it would be a fabulous idea to record it for the show. After he agreed to let us record the date we decided we would meet up.

We met up at some food court in a shopping plaza. This guy looked like a blonde version of Michael Jackson. He wasn't very attractive but maybe he had a good personality. WRONG! From the moment we met the guy was a douche bag! He belittled both my friend and I any chance he got. He was telling us that we should dress better, dye our hair a different color, get our teeth fixed. I couldn't tell if he was just being a douche for the camera or was just that much of an asshole.

For some reason he wanted to take me back to his place but wanted to show me these boats on lake or something. He had to go to the bathroom and we said we would wait. Only thing is we didn't wait and we tried our best to ditch him. I thought it would make for some good drama for the show, and I could give him a taste of his own medicine. We ended up successfully ditching him. Things slightly backfired as he said he didn't care that we left he only wanted to take me back to his place so he could fuck me.

I couldn't think of a way to logically edit it to where I looked better and not like an asshole who ditched him. I also couldn't think of a way to make him look nicer. I wasn't comfortable manipulating the story to get more views. I also didn't wanna just show him as a complete asshole on the off chance he wasn't and was just doing it for the attention. So I ended up cutting all of his parts completely out. Was a tough call but I felt like I was doing the right thing.

The final guy that I would end up dating for a while would more or less be a summer fling type of guy. This guy's name was Brian, and to be honest I can't really describe him or how we met. I just remember him being around twenty-one because he was able to buy alcohol when carded. We just hung out almost every day and I remember getting free food at this one diner because he knew the owner. I ended recording a few of our dates for my show but never really used any of the footage in the final product. We were very close to making a sex tape because one time we were fooling around and decided to start recording. We didn't go all the way, but I thought about releasing the full footage. I thought it could propel my career to the next level and get people talking about me. That is how celebrities were doing it, but I wasn't even close to being famous for anything aside from having nearly three hundred subscribers on my entertainment channel. That isn't very impressive today but back in the day that was quite an accomplishment for a nobody. I decided against it because he wanted to become a pharmacist and I couldn't be the one to ruin his career. That he could do on his own.

Our relationship was mostly just let's get together hang out, and fool around. Neither one of us really cared about the other. Everyday that I was with him I knew it would eventually end because it felt empty. We were invited to a party but when we got there, the place was filled with people drinking and smoking pot. I was not at all comfortable so I just walked right out the door and didn't give it a second thought. He stayed for a few minutes but then came out to make sure I was alright. He didn't want to stay at the party if I was uncomfortable. That was the first time he seemed to actually show any kind of concern. Although a few days later we decided not to see each other anymore. That would be the last I would hear from him as well. I don't know if me not wanting to stay at the party had anything to do with us breaking up, but I didn't care. I needed to change my focus. A relationship wasn't going to be in the cards for me and I was releasing different video blogs, and random comedy skits that were getting a few hundred to a few thousand views each. I had to start thinking about what was the next step was for me. I decided that I really wanted to travel somewhere. It felt important to me to want do discover more about myself.

# CHAPTER 8 – Just an Irish lad

Nikki and I had been talking about taking some sort of vacation together. We had both recently lost grandparents within the prior year. One of the things that we both had in common was that in our family ancestry there was a heavy amount of Irish. We had ancestors that were still coming over from Ireland in the early 1900s. The choice was clear for the both of us and we mutually decided on Ireland. I have an aunt that does family genealogy for a living. She was able to let us know that we both still had relatives that were living in Ireland. She unfortunately didn't have contact information for these people but it was still a very cool thing to know that we had relatives there. Those were some of the areas that we would be interested in exploring so we started to plan a trip around that information.

The worst part about the whole thing was trying to get off work during the holiday shopping season. We were being paid enough to afford a trip during the off peak travel season. We would have to work nearly twice as much to go any other time of the year.

This was wonderful for us. I wanted to travel to at least one other country in my lifetime and to be able to do it before I was twenty felt like an accomplishment. This was the first time that we were both doing something for ourselves. Nobody was helping us plan this, nobody was helping us pay. We worked for it.

We had a five hour flight which I thought for sure would take longer but surprisingly the time flew by. Oh look at that I just made a pun out of that! I think most of that was our amazement that we were able to actually drink alcohol while on the plane. I guess it was one of those things where you are technically in an Irish aircraft so once in air it is like being on Irish soil. We kicked back a couple of over-priced drinks and then shared laughs over a card game.

Our first few nights of our trip were going to be spent in Killarney. We both passed out in the hotel room before our dinner that night. I guess jet lag was a real thing after all. While walking down to the dining room, we were talking to a nice retired older gentleman. He was in our tour group that we were a part of and he was asking us if we watched the rugby game. Evidently on the bus ride from the airport to the hotel he was sitting next to us and talking about rugby. I think we were both just so infatuated with the scenery and looking out the window to take everything in that we completely ignored him. He was traveling alone because his wife had passed on a few years prior and they used to go to Ireland for their anniversary. He wanted to continue the tradition. The sentiment was very nice but I felt like an ass for not really being too empathetic. We pretended that we watched the game and enjoyed our first night by making a new friend for this trip. There were many parts of our trip that we would actually end up hanging out with this gentleman, but we didn't want him to be our focus.

There was a club or a pub next to our hotel that was hosting a goth party that night. We went to the nearest department store to get some accessories. We bought some black eyeliner, nail polish, lipstick, choker collar, and some spiky arm cuffs. We wanted to at least somewhat look the part. It was a much different atmosphere. We instantly felt more comfortable unlike being in an American club. The dance floor wasn't overwhelmingly crowded and most while the music was pumping loud it wasn't going to make us deaf. There was free shots and glow sticks. I remember drinking a bit and Nikki and I possibly making out then making out with some couple that thought her and I were  a thing.

They both had matching red and black hair with purple streaks on opposite sides. I think one of them had a tongue piercing. We stayed way longer than we had planned and just crashed on our bed the second we got back to the hotel room.

We would be spending a second night in Killarney and this time we were actually just going to take it easy. We did some sight seeing and went to go catch a movie in the afternoon. We went to another pub that night. That one was having a pop music dance night so it was right up our alley. There was this cute guy that was flirting with me, so I decided to talk to him and get to know him a bit. He was a nice guy with ginger hair and green eyes. Quite an Irish looking lad. I didn't know much about him other than he was attractive, my age, and had an accent to die for.  He invited us both back to his flat which wasn't too far from our hotel. He had a few friends over and thought we would all hit it off and we can enjoy a night of craic. I had a pen pal at the time from Ireland who had used the expression before and I knew it was a slang word for having fun or gossiping with friends. Looking back it was a rather stupid thing to do but we were young and dumb and that was the sort of thing you did.

I knew that nothing beyond just a hook up could happen with this guy if that even. Being back at his flat, I got to know him a bit better and the more I talked to him the more infatuated with him I became. I think it was mostly falling for the guy with the accent type of thing. Unless I saw him for two weeks each year there was no way a relationship would work. He offered to make us some drinks and of course we weren't turning that down.

After a few drinks we started playing truth or dare and one of his friends dared him to kiss me. I laughed it off like I was shy and embarrassed by the idea but he went in for it. I was completely lost in that moment. I tuned out everyone else in the room and was just so focused on that moment. Nikki was taking a few silly pics with the others, meanwhile this guy took me back to his room. We kissed, talked, and drank a bit more. I think Nikki was starting to feel like she drank too much so we ended up stumbling back to the hotel. Before I left this guy gave me his contact information for me to keep in touch.

Nikki and I passed out the moment we got back to our room. We woke up the next morning and I think she had a hang over. I had been drinking water at the party in between drinks so I think that may have helped me avoid a hangover. I however couldn't remember much of what happened. We had just one more night in Killarney before we moved on to our next destination. Nikki, spent most of the day at the hotel and I did some sight seeing and exploring. When I got back I decided to do some relaxing myself. I went to the hotel pool and went for a swim. This guy in the pool kept swimming around me. He finally got the nerve to strike up a conversation. We went to the lower end of the pool where they had the massaging jets in the whirlpool style hot tub. He was also visiting Ireland and his story almost mirrored mine. He was also traveling with his best friend who was a female. We both had the same astrological sign, born days apart. The only differences were part of his ancestry was Italian and he was from Canada. I had lost track of time and forgotten that I was supposed to meet back up with Nikki. I wished him well in his travels and parted ways. Before heading back up to my room I had noticed that locker room had a sauna. I had never been in a sauna and I figured there was a first time for everything. I stripped down to just my towel and hung the rest of my stuff in my locker. There were a few other guys in the sauna. They were mostly older men and we all just sat there a steam filled silence.

They started to leave the sauna one after another. At some point I was alone, or so I thought. It turns out my new Canadian friend was in there.

Neither one of us spoke a word, because I assumed sauna etiquette was just not to talk to one another. Evidently he was the last person in the pool and it was already that late. We were the only two people in the sauna. The pool was now closed and the locker room was empty. He looked me in the eye and he slowly undid his towel. I wasn't sure what was going on but I figured I would just sit here and relax anyway. He started to slowly rub himself and was getting slightly aroused. I wanted not to stare but he was an attractive guy. I still had on my but was fighting back getting aroused myself. He inched a bit closer to me and put his leg up on me and started rubbing my thiigh with his foot. As he was doing that he was full on erect and he inched his foot closer to my crotch. My towel slipped off as he was rubbing his foot against my crotch. I was fully aroused and enjoying every second of this. He leans over a bit closer and we start to kiss. Before things start to go too far, I pull back and pretend that I heard a noise. I told him I thought someone was coming. He gets paranoid and things stop. We walk out of the sauna together and get dressed. While getting dressed we exchanged contact info to keep in touch.

Nikki, was quite upset when I got back to the hotel room, but not for the reasons I thought. Evidently, she had posted a blog summarizing our crazy party. Mutual friends of ours were tearing us apart for some reason. A couple of our friends had been annoyed that we were going on this trip. Almost as if we were bragging about it. Honestly we may have been but we were proud. However that was no reason to start bullshit for no reason. I told her to just block them and be done with it. No point in carrying on with senseless drama. This was our trip and we were going to spend it the way we wanted. In a way I was glad she was so upset about the blog, because I had no idea how to even tell her about my sauna experience. We ended up calling it a night early and moved on to the next part of our trip.

We spent the next few days buying clothes on clearance at Dunne's. Every time we came across one we had to stop. For one reason or another that was becoming our go to store. We did some sight seeing over the next few days and stopping at various cities and towns along the way. We went to some farm for tea and scones, went to some pottery making class, went to some old winery, and abandoned castle type thing, and quite a few things in between. There was some sort of dolphin in a town called Dingle, that was a huge deal. We got to Galway, and that was another fun city. However fun soon turned to rather unusual, and an awkward situation that depended on Nikki saving me.

After we explored the town we got back to the hotel. Nikki and I went to the hotel's bar and played cards and just were chatting about life events. We had a couple of drinks just to sip on. Not enough to get us drunk or anything like that. Shortly after she decides she wants to call it a night. I had told her I would be up in a few minutes. I was going to order another drink and maybe a little snack, but that she could go if she was tired and I wouldn't make much noise when I got to the room. She left me and I was mostly alone in the hotel bar minus the bartender. As I'm getting ready these two older gentlemen are walking in and bump into me. They apologize and feel bad about almost knocking me over that they want to buy me a drink. Without asking me they order me an Irish whiskey.

I walk back over to the couch that I was sitting on and they both sit on opposite sides of me. They were both very attractive men. One slightly looked like a mix between David Beckham, and George Clooney and had to be somewhere in his 40's. They were in amazing shape as well. The other guy was maybe in his 50's with more of a Sean Connery look to him. I always have had a thing for older guys and anyone that gives me attention, I am prone to liking.

They were from Ireland but on the opposite side and were on some sort of business trip. They didn't come off as gay to me, so it seemed like they were just up for some casual conversation. I had never had whiskey prior to this and I didn't quite realize how potent it was. I was drinking it rather slowly and it came in a rather sizable little glass.

They were slowly getting to know more and more about me. I avoided answering questions that I thought were too personal. Things such as my relationship status, and if I liked men or women. I just kept it to topics of movies, music, or whatever current event was going on. I just felt uneasy talking about my personal life. They kept getting a bit closer to me as I drank more, but I thought nothing of it. They called for another round of drinks which meant I was having more whiskey. I didn't want anymore, I wasn't near my alcohol limit. I just didn't really like the taste. I had expressed that they didn't have to do that, but they insisted it was all good. The conversation started going from casual to near sexual. They were starting to make dirty jokes about the bartender. Then they were talking about this time they picked up this lad walking home from a pub, and told him he could ride in the car naked.

Nikki, had started to send me a few text messages. Which I really was trying not to answer because they cost something like 25 or 50 cents per message because of the international rate. One of the guys pointed it out to me that, would probably cost a lot of money to send messages. Now I am starting to think that these guys didn't want me to be using my phone for some reason. I was starting to get this really uncomfortable vibe. I had told them I was ready to call it a night and they ordered me another whiskey and said I could stay for a bit longer. A few minutes pass. They started to get a bit closer to me and started putting their hands on me, one on my leg another on my shoulder. They were talking more about what they did with the guy they picked up from the pub before. They pulled over somewhere and gave him a blowjob. Then they had a threesome and gifted the guy a few dollars as a tip so he could buy himself some nice things. I look over to the bar area to see the bartender is nowhere to be found. I was thinking if I could get his attention, and have him come over to clean up the area a bit, then I could make my escape. Thoughts of what to do next were racing through my head. These guys were both very attractive, but the alcohol was also starting to cloud my judgment. I was at the point where I was curious to see where this would go, but I also was very uncomfortable hearing their previous story. I came to the point where I just stopped drinking the whiskey because I didn't want to become any more impaired and make a potentially regrettable decision.

They noticed that I stopped drinking for a few minutes. They told me we could all go up to their room and finish everything up there. There was no pressure, and we could just talk some more. I told them I'd go back to their room with them. Worst case scenario I could pull a fire alarm in the hall before we got to the room and pretend I bumped into it by being slightly drunk. Actually that was exactly what I was planning to do. I knew there was fire alarms close to the elevators. The elevators also had cameras so I knew they weren't likely to try something in the elevator. I figured once we got to their floor I would plan my escape. They were staying two floors above me, so I could make a run down the fire escape and get a hold of Nikki during the chaos.

We got on the elevator and things were so quiet. That elevator ride felt like an eternity. I heard a ding and was afraid to look at the floor number. I look up and we aren't at the correct floor. The hallway illuminates the elevator with an almost heavenly glow. I hear a familiar voice saying, "Oh my God! There you are, I've been trying to get a hold of you for the last hour or so." It was Nikki! We were actually on my floor. I wasn't out of the woods yet. I didn't know what to say or do. I just gave her a blank stare. She must have seen the worry in my eyes. She said "Baby, I was ready for bed and was coming down to get you. I didn't see your pocket knife you must have it on you. I was bringing you mine just in case. It was getting late and I was worried about you." I went along with it and pretended she was my girlfriend. "Oh honey, I love you so much. I was just getting ready to come back to the room. Nikki, pushed a random button on the elevator and pretended we were going to that floor. She came closer to me and I wrapped my arm around her and gave her a slight kiss. The guys just looked at me and didn't say a word. They got off on their floor and walked out of the elevator. I'm not sure if they were putting their plan to a halt or if the whole pocket knife thing scared them off. Whatever it was it worked. When they got off Nikki, looked at me and asked me about what happened. As we walked back to the room I explained everything to her and was so glad she showed up at just the right time. Thankfully I didn't have to pull a fire alarm.

I am not sure what would have happened if she didn't show up, or if my alarm plan backfired. I am just glad that I didn't have to find out. They went from being very attractive to freaking me out in a matter of minutes. That night taught me an important lesson about keeping my guard up and being aware of my surroundings. Especially when in a foreign country. It wasn't anything near like the sauna, where it was actually a mutual thing and someone that made me slightly more comfortable. I got a good vibe from the sauna guy. These guys not at all. Something about it made me feel like I was violated and I just snuggled up with Nikki for comfort.

The rest of the trip was back to more fun. We got to stay in a castle and I swear to you I had some sort of paranormal experience there. I can't really explain it but I felt like I was being attacked by a violent spirit. I wasn't dreaming and I was wide awake. Nikki woke up during it and she felt like she was thrown off the bed as she was trying to make sure I was alright. I didn't kick her, or make any sudden movements that would throw off her balance. She got back to me and we both calmed down. I thought maybe I was having a violent dream, maybe I was in that weird stage of being awake but still dreaming. Maybe it was my imagination playing tricks on me. Something felt off about that night and I had trouble falling back asleep.

We went through a few more places and then we ended up staying a few nights in Dublin. We were mostly partied out at this point. I think we went to a karaoke. Did some of the traditional sight seeing. Towards our last few nights we just had one more night just celebrating in our hotel. We bought alcohol and chocolate chip cookies and some other random things. We went out in style and slept most of the plane ride home. It was a fun trip. We got to bond and make our friendship stronger. It was important to both of us and I wouldn't have wanted to share it with anyone else.

# CHAPTER 9 - The reality of love

After our adventure in Ireland, Nikki and I, got back into our normal routine. We were both working all the time. I ended up actually getting a management job and was doing that for a bit. I ended up meeting a guy and getting back into modeling as well. I was also at a point where I was starting to do a second season of my self made reality show. I hadn't done anything with it in almost a year. My camera had broken a few months prior to the Ireland trip and most of my money was going to that trip. The idea of dropping another three hundred dollars for a decent camcorder was not in the cards. I ended up investing in a new one a few months after coming back. Now back to the show! Rather than being random clips that were put together I was doing little recaps and giving my thoughts like you see on actual reality shows. The dating life and trying to get some good clips for the show would not be a good mix.

I was dating one guy, but he wasn't all too memorable. We had a casual thing going on and he wasn't a very good boyfriend. He would frequently bail on plans and have some sort of excuse to follow. He stopped answering my phone calls, so I started talking to another guy. This guy's name was Drake.

Drake was an incredibly good looking guy. He had this ivory soft pale skin, fashionably styled jet black hair, plump luscious full lips and was just gorgeous. He was about two years older than I was. He was going to college for something but I can't recall what. He also was a big poetry writer. His poems shared both the good and bad. He had been through some heartache in life and you could see through his writings that he was doing his best to recover.

Our first date was very laid back but we hit it off right from the start. It was also uncharted territory. My attraction to him was instant and it was more than just a physical thing. All we did on our first date was go for a walk along a nature trail. It wasn't much but when we got to a waterfall at the end of the trail we kissed. In that kiss was the first time I felt like I was actually feeling a spark and connecting with someone's soul. This wasn't just making out with another guy and never being kissed.

Drake and I would date over several months. A lot of my friends were getting to know him and they just adored him. Around this same time I had another friend who making suggestions for my videos. When I hung out with this person they would be coming up ways to stir up drama. This person decided to sleep over one night and I had another friend call me at around 3 am in the morning one night. She had some sort of problem. She had an argument with her sister or her mother and I honestly just didn't want to be bothered at that time. I had to be up for work in a few hours so I snapped on her. This woke up the friend who encouraged drama and he grabbed the camcorder and started recording everything. My friend thought it would make for some good clips for the show. He then directed me to call her back and start even more drama. For some dumb reason I thought that was an incredible idea. The thrill of getting more views outweighed the benefit of having a good friend. I was such an idiot at that time. Drake was on the fence about me doing these video blogs and clips. He was fine taking photos with me and sharing them on social media, but he didn't want much to be a part of my videos. He was more concerned about getting negative comments. For every fan I had, I had another person bashing me for no reason and trolling my page.

I took a break from doing anything with video blogging or my so called reality show. I was starting to have strong feelings for Drake. Our relationship would get taken to the next level one night and it was mostly magical. Not exactly the way I wanted things to go, but overall the dynamic of our relationship would change for a bit.

We had a romantic night in and I am not quite sure what even led to everything. I had some candles going and we were listening to whatever was on the radio. I had these red satin sheets on the bed. As we were laying in the bed together we started to kiss and caress each other and sensually strip each other of our clothing. We pressed our naked bodies against each other and it felt like our flesh was two ships sailing on a velvety satin sea. Rubbing up against each other skin to skin was getting us both aroused. We continued to kiss and our lips touching and our hands exploring each other's skin. He grabbed me and he nibbled on my ear and whispered that he was "ready". I kissed down from his neck to his chest, licking his nipple and leading a trail of sweet kisses to the tip of his erect penis. I wrapped my tongue and mouth around his shaft and started to tease him a bit. His eyes were rolling back in his head and I went to the tip of his penis and then resumed kissing further down. I kissed down his legs and right to his feet. I started kissing his feet and then began licking his toes. He returned the favor to me by following my path.

He asked me if I was comfortable with going all the way and me fucking him. Every bit of me was ready. This was the moment I had been waiting for and he was the person I was waiting to do it with. I didn't have this kind of chemistry with anyone else. I grabbed some lubricant out of the dresser and I fingered him a little to get him loose and ready. Everything was so perfect as I was getting ready to slowly penetrate him. He guided me in slowly and let out a couple of moans. I did a few slight thrusts and he told me it felt, "incredible". He wanted me to go harder and faster, so I did. We kissed as I thrusted and you could feel the magic in the air. After a few minutes I was ready to cum. He told me he wanted me to cum inside of him as he would jerk off. We both hit our peak at the same time and ejaculated in unison. This was the first time that I had felt anything like that and I felt incredible. He went to go smoke a cigarette because evidently that is a thing you do after incredible sex.

We fell asleep shortly after that and in the middle of the night he wanted to talk to me. He told me that he enjoyed the sex and everything but he wasn't sure if he was ready to do it often. He told me the only other person he had sex with was his Uncle just a few months prior. He said it was a mutual thing but he felt that his Uncle still violated and manipulated him into doing it.

I had no idea what to even think about that. A lot of his poetry hinted at some sort of trauma. If he regretted doing that with his Uncle, then would he later regret doing things with me? It was a lot to process. I didn't know much about dealing with other people's trauma, but I told him I would be patient and wait. If it was something that he needed to build into then that was fine. Sex wasn't important to me one way or the other. I just didn't want him to be comparing what he says was a good experience with me to one he would rather forget with his Uncle. It was a few weeks before we would have sex again or even do anything sexual. I was still lingering on what he said to me. Each time we would have sex would still feel amazing. I tried to be more passionate and make it feel more intimate in any way I could. A gentle massage of the back with some warm body oil to loosen up the muscles and help him relax. Things that would help him be more comfortable and just feel secure with me. That is one thing he longed for was feeling safe and secure. He had a ton of issues and I wanted him to feel like he could forget about his problems and be at peace with me.

He wrote poetry about our relationship. Often the themes were of being in a good place. He often wrote about our sex life and how now he is in a place of ecstasy and pure bliss. No longer did he have fears about being intimate with someone. I guess my patience, and delicacy in the bedroom was working and helping him through some of his issues. Over the next few weeks things would get better for us and he would be a lot more comfortable being intimate.

At one point we were asked to do a couples photo shoot. Someone had reached out to me on my social media page and was interested in doing an erotic couples photo shoot.

We agreed to do the photo shoot and thought it would be a wonderful way to bring us closer together, and nice time capsule of our relationship. The photo shoot itself went well. A lot of the photos turned out gorgeous. They were mostly just us in some various poses. On a couch in a front of a fire place about to share a steamy kiss with my shirt ripped open. Kissing on a dock in front of a lake while embracing nude. Shot of us wearing swim trunks sitting on the dock with our feet in the water holding hands but shot from overhead. Then there were some more erotic photos where we were aroused but they weren't pornographic and still artistic. It was a shoot to just show all facets of a gay couple in love. I had received a horrible haircut right before and the photographer got offended when I got critical of how my hair looked in some of the photos. It wasn't saying anything about his skill or talent, it was me being self conscious about how I looked. The photographer offered us to stay the night and do more work the next day.

During the shoot there was an assistant that was helping with some of the more provocative poses. He was an older male somewhere in his fifties. A lot of the photo shoot was improvised and it was to mostly capture our raw emotion. The assistant was very pushy and quite a bit too hands on. He was practically a fluffer who was trying to massage  or touch us the right way to get us more aroused. I understood his role but during the shoot it gave me some odd vibes. A little bit after the shoot he came into the room where we were staying and he was completely naked. He started talking to us about how we enjoyed the shoot. He was telling us that it turned out amazing. Things got a bit stranger when he was going into detail of how it turned him on and some of the things he would have liked to see us do. He kept talking perverted and dirty and was trying to convince us to have sex in front of him. To sweeten the deal he was rubbing himself and getting aroused. The whole thing was not at all professional and to be honest it was rather repulsive. I do like older guys but at my choosing and if you are going to make an advance at me there has to be some chemistry. In this case there wasn't and it was downright creepy. I told Drake, that we were leaving right away. I turned down the assistant and his offer and went to go tell the photographer we were leaving.

The photographer didn't have much to say and just let us go after finishing up. He was a bit upset that we didn't want to stay for another day. He also was a bit mad at us because he didn't believe his assistant was being a pig. As part of our deal we got to keep some of the raw photos, got our pay and would be emailed some of the final edited images. I didn't care, I just wanted to get out of there. I had been in some weird situations before and I knew my boyfriend had been in some worse ones.

Some time went on and the dynamic of our relationship was changing. I still cared a lot about him, but it felt like the honeymoon phase of our relationship was dwindling. We still had a good connection but there was some small things here and there that were building into some bigger issues. One of the things was he liked to show off how intelligent he was. He used big words often and if I'd use a bigger word he would congratulate me in a snarky way. Then he would put me down if I didn't know how to do something or enough information about a particular subject. I'd often hear phrases like, "Oh my God, you had biology class, how do you not know this?" He was also getting to be very jealous and quite controlling. He wanted to hang out with my friends but I wasn't allowed to hang out with his friends. He could talk to other guys but I couldn't talk to other guys.

We started getting into some small arguments about these things. I would give my thoughts on something and he would turn it around on me and say that I was being mean and not taking his feelings into consideration. I was being pretty lenient and fair and letting him get his way. It came to a point where I just thought I was being manipulating my emotions. He was so good at playing a victim, that no matter what I said or did I was wrong.

Things were getting out of hand. The friend that was telling me what to do for my video blogs suggested that I start video recording some of the calls because it would make for good drama for the show. I foolishly listened and did just that. I had recorded an episode where we were hanging out for his birthday. It was the first time that he let me record him. We had a good time and things seemed fine. Then we got right back into arguing. The one episode I left things rather vague. I shows us having a good time together, but left out all the arguing. I decided the best thing to do would be to break up with him. I broke up with him over the phone and recorded things, and then just me crying over the decision afterwards.

I told him that I couldn't handle how emotional he had been lately and that he should seek some professional help because I felt I was being treated poorly. I couldn't bring myself to make him look like a bad guy for the show. I left out almost everything and just basically said we broke up and I was upset about it. I didn't realize it still made me look like a victim which is exactly what he was doing to me. I did my best to try to present it in a way where neither of us looked like the bad guy. He stopped talking to me for a while.

It wasn't till about a year later that we actually tried to rekindle things. I went to a concert with another friend and afterwards we all met up at this diner. Him and I went out to his car to talk about things. We had some alone time and I apologized for making some of the mistakes I did. We snuggled up and started to kiss. Things still felt the same as before but without the arguing and the problems. After a few minutes of making out we went back into the diner to meet our friends we had with us and we acted as if nothing happened. Both of our friends were on to us because we could not stop flirting or stay apart from each other. We spent the remainder of the night secluding ourselves from the group and just snuggling up next to each other. When our night ended we exchanged a hug and a kiss. We held onto each other tightly and left on a positive note. I know in our hearts we both wanted to get back together but in my mind I knew it wasn't the right thing. We slowly drifted apart from that point.

Right before that magical dinner date and shortly after our breakup I got involved with someone else. This guy was possibly the worst guy I ever dated. He isn't much worth mentioning. He was basically the very definition of a rebound and for some reason I was blinded by him. I really just wanted to show Drake, that I could move on and find better. Only I didn't find better I found worse. I'll make this short because he isn't worth the few paragraphs I am already wasting on him.

He was wonderful to all my friends and family. Total sweetheart. We dated for a couple of months and he wanted me to move in with him. He told me that his mother was sick, and needed care. So I moved to the other side of the state to help him take care of his mother or so I thought. Turns out everything he said about his mother being sick was a complete lie. She wasn't much sick, just a fat bitch that was a piece of shit and had a grudge against me.

He showed his true colors and had his mom wait on him hand and foot. I mean here this guy was twenty-two and his mother was doing everything for him. One time I said he could do something himself and she flipped her shit on me. He also started becoming a bit of a prick and didn't care much of what happened to me. One night I walked to the store to pick up some groceries and he "accidentally" locked me out. So I slept on the front porch until his sister came over in the middle of the night to let me in because he fell asleep.

I was only there a few weeks but I started spending every night at this bowling alley to just get away from him. I befriended this elderly woman named, Ethel. She was a lovely woman and told me I would be a fucking idiot if I decided to stay with this guy.

The final straw was one night when we got into a fight about I am not even sure what it was about to be honest with you. I had told him that I thought he was lazy, unmotivated, and he needed to grow up. He wasn't very happy with my critique. I had arranged to get picked up to move back home. I didn't tell him any of this or that I was planning to leave. I went upstairs to start packing my shit and get everything together. His mother came up the stairs and started pounding on the door. She was shouting and yelling at me. I told her to get out of my face. She all of a sudden took a swing at me but I saw it coming and blocked it and grabbed her wrist. I told her if she tried it again her fat ass would go flying down the stairs. She turned right around and walked down the stairs. I wanted her to trip so badly but sadly she did not. Then the douche bag comes marching up the stairs because his mother claimed that I was being mean to her.

He started yelling at me and telling me that I needed to get out. He was watching me pack and demanding I didn't take this or that and a lot of the things he was yelling about were things I owned. I told him he needed to back off. He started throwing some of my stuff out the window to the outside. I grabbed the last few things and walked down the stairs. I went out on the porch to wait for my ride and he locked the door behind me. I could hear him and his mother the entire time talking about how ungrateful I was and what he was going to do to get back at me. His sister ended up coming over to talk to me and she was the only sensible one. She sat there and waited with me on the porch to make sure I was safe and that they didn't cause anymore unnecessary drama. She kept apologizing for their behavior and how she felt truly embarrassed. This was the worst guy I ever encountered until I had a guy attempt to drug me and take advantage of me but I will get to that a bit later. Gotta keep you interested in this story somehow!

# CHAPTER 10 – Reality Bites

The following year I was at a point where I wasn't sure what I wanted to do next. I was at a point where I was around twenty years old. I went through this odd almost emo phase where I was trying to hold onto my teenage years because I didn't want that time to slip away. It was something I could never live through again. I heard of this website that had recently started where you could do live video blogs and people would watch you. You could have various people be co-hosts and be on cam with you. You could be on cam and chat with people in the room. It wasn't a sexual type of site but it was one where you could play music, perform skits, or just live stream a video blog. I started doing that and I did not expect people would actually start to follow me.

The thing was I could actually sing and tried my hands out at being in a band. I couldn't play in instrument so I was mostly a vocalist. I tried with a few different people and wrote some songs. As much as I enjoyed doing shows in coffee houses I just felt doing that and getting nowhere wasn't my thing. So my approach to doing the live video blogging was just to see what other people who were popular were doing and to see what I could learn from them. Only instead of learning I was critical.

I would often go onto my channel and start bashing or talking shit about whoever was popular that week. I was saying the things that people were thinking and I had found what my persona would be. I wasn't afraid to stir the pot and I would sometimes piss off a lot of their fans. People would come into my show and they would just bash me and leave me all sorts of hates. I had my own group of fans that would destroy them upon entering. It was a hostile environment and cyber bullying wasn't a thing at that time. It was working for me though. People thought I was funny and a lot of the times I would even get messages from some of the people I made fun of but in a positive way. They took it as me roasting them and felt flattered. I was starting to become more popular on the site, a few times even being a featured video blogger with my show on the home page. The friend I had from earlier who was telling me what to do in some of my other videos took notice and then wanted to take control of this as well. They kept telling me that I had to be more aggressive, more controversial, and more of a bitch.

This led me to an opportunity at a new concept for an online reality tv show.

Online gaming based of off popular reality shows was a thing for years. Most of them were done via chat rooms or message boards. This was a whole new concept that mixed recorded video diaries, live multi cam video challenges, and multicam video chat feeds. There were times we would get together for challenges, virtual hang out sessions and group chats. All of these things would be recorded and the most dramatic clips would be used for the show. Overall the show flopped hard and the producer didn't even post the whole season online. The show didn't even have an official name and only a few previews surfaced online despite how much time was put into it. The producer stopped paying to host the site and it just sort of vanished. The idea was good on paper but maybe it was a bit ahead of its time. Things like Twitter weren't yet as popular and hashtags and trending topics didn't really exist. Message forums were dying out and social media was changing. That and the show just wasn't that interesting.

I remember I was picked because they were doing a thing with upcoming video bloggers, or wannabe famous people. Some of the other people

145

picked were bloggers I made fun of in the past and that was going to create some controversial moments. Both my friend and the producer wanted me to amp up my personality. They knew I was bitchy but they wanted me to be a bit bitchier. I was at this point playing a character. The overly gay and overly dramatic person that surprisingly nobody liked. The way the show worked was each week we'd be competing to stay in the show. Then a few people would vote on who should be eliminated. Then it came down to those three chosen. The three would do another challenge to stay in the game. The winner would go on and the bottom two would face some sort of weird voting system that I didn't understand.

I was told that when it came to any kind of challenges to find the most ridiculous reason to not participate in it. One time it was something like hit yourself with a whip creamed pie and then use your finger to lick as much off your face. I backed out and said that I was far too pretty and that the whipped cream could clog my pores and my face might break out. Other players tore into me in their video journals and made fun of how over the top I was. I lasted a bit longer than I expected. I think there were twelve players and I was fourth voted out. There was one fat girl who had multiple personalities and she claimed to have some sort of demon inside her. She was the first to go. I can't much remember the other two. I think one quit and the other was too quiet.

To be honest with you I was glad the show flopped and never actually took off. I was presented in such a terrible way. I was playing this character that was the furthest from who I was. It was a terrible idea to do the show. It didn't help me get more popular at all. People actually hated me and I was starting to get a lot of nasty emails and comments. It wasn't like being in wrestling where if you are hated, you are doing your job right. This was just people saying down right nasty things, because of someone they thought I was. I slowly started to drift away from doing live video blogs. I was going to focus on strictly doing stuff that I could edit and upload later. This way I wouldn't deal with all the crazy of a live feed. I cut off all communication with the friend that was wanting to "manage my career". That person was so toxic and gave me a lot of bad advice, and direction and for some reason I was stupid enough to listen. They wanted to have this thing where they had all these ideas but they weren't as good looking as I was, they couldn't act, and they wouldn't get a reaction from people the way I could. Essentially they were using me to act out a part of what they wanted to portray themselves. I didn't feel like that was a healthy thing at all so I stopped talking to them.

The mid to late 2000s and trying to be a "gay entertainer" was difficult to deal with at times. Even though LGBT representation was taking off in movies and TV. People online could be really cruel. I was doing some videos and had some people who looked up to me or admired me. They saw me as this funny good looking guy who didn't much care what people thought and they saw it was ok to be yourself. They didn't see that some people were just damn vicious. Having people say hateful things or getting "death threats" was just insane to me. It was a lot to deal with at times. The other side of it was getting messages of how I inspired someone to come out to their family or that they felt comfortable in their own skin because of me.

There were already a ton of over the top gay video bloggers out there and I didn't want to be that nasty bitchy one. I did my best after the show to just do real videos talking about  things that were important to me and to show. I didn't want to stop being a source of inspiration to those that looked up to me. I just got to a point where I just didn't want to do any kind of videos. I took a break from doing videos for a bit. I stopped checking my channel daily to keep up with comments and messages. I think that was wonderful for my overall mental being for a bit. I didn't have to concern myself with what the haters were saying and I didn't have to try to see what I could do to get more and more views. I no longer cared about becoming famous or getting popular. I went back to the basics and just did videos when I felt like it and not because someone was expecting something on Tuesday night.

During my online video blogging hiatus I ended up meeting a guy. This was not the kind of guy that I actually ever wanted to meet. We met on some sort of dating site and he actually had seen a few of my comedy skits, and video blogs. He said he was a "fan" of my work but was interested in getting to know me. I think his name was Jason. I know he was somewhere in his mid twenties and slightly overweight and kept his hair buzzed short.

I talked to him for a few weeks before agreeing to finally meet up. He handled himself well in online conversations but when I actually met up with him he seemed like he had some sort of mental issues. I couldn't quite pin point it but something was not right about him. The way he looked at me freaked me out instantly. The way he talked to me was borderline sadistic. This was sometime shortly after I turned twenty-one. I just remember us going out to a gay bar together. I still wanted to give him a chance because sometimes first impressions can be wrong. Although in my case they usually are never wrong. If I meet you and something rubs me the wrong way there is usually a reason.

When we were at the bar we both had a few drinks. I remember him ordering me some sort of margarita with the salted rim. One of my friends was at the bar and distracted me for a few minutes with conversation. While my back was turned I wasn't watching my drink which is a rookie mistake to make. Don't ever do it. Like always keep an eye on your drink. I was freshly twenty-one what the hell did I know about this? After catching up with my friend I let him know I had a date to get back to. I turned around and I swear I had my drink on my left side and not my right side. Yet here it was on the right side. I go to take a sip and look at some white powdery stuff floating in my drink. It doesn't look right to me so I pointed it out to him. He swears to me that it must be some of the salt from the rim of the glass and I shouldn't worry about it. Only it wasn't as granulated or white as the salt was. Plus some of the chunks were a bit bigger. This looked like it was some sort of crushed pill. I call over the bartender and I tell him there is something floating in my drink. Jason still is claiming it is salt and starts to argue with the bartender over it. I just ask the bartender if he could dump that one to be safe and I'd pay for another one. Jason seems to be getting frustrated over this.

I start to feel a bit dizzy and I start to think that maybe when I wasn't looking that Jason slipped something in one of my other drinks and I actually drank it. I tell him I am going to the bathroom quickly. He claims he is going to order me another drink and I just tell him that I don't want another one because my stomach is bothering me. He starts to insist I would be fine. I found my friend on the club side of the bar and asked him to come with me. I tell him that I think I might have been drugged and if he could keep an eye on me and possibly take me home later. He agrees and tells me to text him if I need him and he will come right away, but he has to get back to his date. I understood and let him get back to his date. I end up going over to a nearby couch.

I started to feel tired and the room was spinning. I was not sure if there was something in my drink or if I was just so paranoid that my mind was playing tricks on me now. I start to fall asleep on the couch and a few minutes later Jason is on the couch and I am drifting in and out of my waking state. I feel his hands under my shirt but I'm too tired to care. I start drifting out and I can feel his hands going lower towards my crotch. I am completely zoned out at this point and the next thing I see is my friend looking at me while pulling Jason off of me. My shirt is half off and my pants are unbuttoned. Evidently he was trying to blow me in this dark corner of the club where it was dark enough to be discreet. My friend threw Jason to the ground and Jason got up and walked away without saying a word. My friend asks me if I am alright but I am not quite sure what was even going on. He tells me it looks like he was trying to take advantage of me. My friend didn't hear from me so he came to check on me. My friend said he would be taking me home and it looks like he came just in time. I don't know if I had a few too many drinks or if something was in my drink but something was not right there. I was thrilled that my friend was there to save the day because if not I am not sure what would have happened. Would I have been taken advantage of and left there? It wasn't something that I wanted to find out. I never heard from Jason again after that. I went home and I had a message from Jason. He was trying to say he wanted to make sure I was safe and that we both had a bit too much too drink. I just blocked him without so much as a reply. I heard through the grapevine a few years later that he had issues with drugs and may have overdosed. My first impression of something being off with him was correct. I hope that if those rumors are true. That he got his life together, or found peace in some way.

I made my video hiatus a little bit longer because I didn't even want to think of him watching my videos. I knew that wasn't the way to think so I eventually started doing more videos because I couldn't hide from him or it. I got lucky I had a friend who was there for me and I wasn't taken advantage of. Not everybody gets that lucky. I counted my blessings and moved on. I went on a nice few dates with other guys after that. Couldn't let one bad seed ruin the fun. I wasn't going to dwell on it any longer. At the same time I ended up doing some local acting again and getting cast in some murder mystery type of play. It was a very small role but it was a nice break from doing videos and helped me transition into my next new found passion.

# CHAPTER 11 – You gotta laugh

The previous year was just as much of a roller coaster as you could get. I had that appearance on that failed reality show. I was going to a lot of concerts and clubs and enjoying life. I tried out for several game shows but didn't get a call back. I rekindled a romance with my ex briefly. Met a guy that tried to take advantage of me. Right before that weirdo I also dated a guy that stayed with me for a bit of time, but he took advantage of my generosity. Long story short he just had nowhere else to go and would stay with whatever guy would put up with him for long enough. He was beyond emotionally manipulative. I'm going to actually touch upon this in a bit. There is a whole series of drama that actually flows together and it makes more sense to the story to present it a bit later. Anyway the point is my life was chaotic. I was thinking that it was time to start getting back into wrestling but I wanted to try my hand at doing comedy first. This would be a good thing because getting even more comfortable in front of an audience would be wonderful for my charisma.

I got involved with a local improv and comedy workshop group. I came across an ad online for a local classifieds site. I was like well this sounds like it will be a cool thing to try. The leader of the group was allegedly a semi regular on the NYC comedy scene. The problem with that is it is such a big city and there are thousands of comics and not very many stand out. They all sort of blend together and there are a ton of comedy clubs. So you could have a following of 4 people at some club in the basement of a bar and say you are a regular on the New York comedy scene.

The improv group was a fantastic way for me to learn about what worked and what didn't work in doing comedy skits. We would be given these scenarios and have either loose scripts or have to improvise the whole thing. We'd get feedback on what was working and what fell flat. We also started working on our own material to get the same kind of feedback. Sometimes I'd write what I thought was a fantastic set only to not realize I repeated something or overused a joke and it wasn't as funny. My material was also not as easy to critique. I was more of a story driven comic. I'd tell funny stories, and would rely on my body language or tone of voice to really set up the laugh. I wasn't the type of comic that could write one liners or have a rolling punch line type of thing. Not to say I totally couldn't but it just wasn't my style or my niche. There were hundreds of male comics in my area already doing a string of short jokes with random punchlines. That just wasn't for me. I found a niche that I could make fun of myself and the gay lifestyle and that would be my niche. Most of the places I'd perform were actually in front of mostly straight audiences so it would surprisingly work. I just didn't want that to be all I did. Like how sometimes all female comics do is just bitch about men, and black comics make black jokes. I didn't want to be stereotyped into that category so I tried to mix it up when I could.

I eventually left the group because I felt I was ready to start taking on my own gigs. I worked my ass off going to any open mics that I could. Sometimes I'd drive near two hours to just get in a five minute set at an open mic. I was doing what I could to get my name out there. A lot of the people that went to open mics were mostly other comics and their friends. Although sometimes you'd get lucky and a few club owners would be in the audience scouting someone to perform on an opening act for one of the main performers. Those are the people I wanted to impress.

As I did more and more of these open mics I would be taking notes in the back of my comedy notebook which had my set list in it. I'd notate what others were doing and what was working and how they'd change it up to match the crowd, or what was falling flat with that particular audience. I always hated going first because reading an audience is one of the hardest things to do, especially to do it on the spot and to have to change things on the fly. These were all things that would come with experience. I think it was around the time Michael Jackson died although I could be thinking of another beloved celebrity. Someone put all Michael Jackson jokes in their set and nobody laughed at a single one of their jokes. Any other time that may have been funny but people were devastated by his death and evidently "too soon" was a real thing. I know that is something I didn't want to do.

After doing a few open mics I ended up getting booked on my first show so it would be my official debut where I would have more than five minutes. I think I had twelve minutes and that didn't seem like much but still was quite a bit of time to fill for a rookie.

I was painfully nervous and terribly anxious. I brought a few friends with me and they were my street team. We posted flyers around town to get people to come to the show. I also made my own flyers that had my contact info and links to social media sites. This particular club was in a four star hotel and everything in the hotel seemed fancier than it actually was. We spammed the hotel with my flyers. We left them on tables in the lounge area in and around the club, in the travel brochure area, the hotel lobby, the front desk. I was determined to get a few fans from this or at least people to potentially be interested. I had to separate from my friends and go into the "green room" which was an empty conference room that had a small snack platter and tiny bottles of water. We had to go in there to go over some of the hotel and club rules. There were certain things we weren't allowed to say or do, but otherwise it was mostly off limits. They also explained to us exactly what order we would be going in and what the wrap up cue was. This guy would be sitting in the back of the room with a small tiny flashlight and he would flash it a few times as if it was morse code and that meant we had about a minute left to wrap things up. The only problem with that was, how the fuck were you supposed to see the light? I ended up setting a timer on my phone and disabling text messages and calls so I would feel a vibration in my pocket. I figured it would work the same. I could start the timer while they were doing my intro before I walked on stage.

There was a tv in the green room that was live streaming the comedy show. I think I was fourth or fifth our of ten people that were performing. Watching the first few people and how hilarious they were made me more uncomfortable. I thought for sure I would just fail miserably. The time came for me to be called on. We all got to write out own intros and I made mine sound like I was this well experienced guy and that it would be this borderline controversial set. I tried to avoid doing anything political because I hated political jokes but I ended up making one anyway because I was trying to get around one of the banned words. We couldn't say the word cunt. So I did my intro and my first few bits and in the middle set up for that joke. I ended up doing this joke about the word cunt without saying it but making a rhyme with a similar sounding word and the name of a certain person that was very well disliked at the time and the crowd ate it up. It was at that moment that my fears were completely wiped away. The crowd cheered and applauded and hollered in a good way and I just stood there and let it all sink in. I waited for it to die down before I moved onto my next bit and it helped me be comfortable with the rest of the set.

My friends came up to me after the set to congratulate me and in the lobby people were walking around and a lot of people enjoyed my set. I met this nice couple in their late twenties and they thought I had an incredible stage presence and wanted to get a picture with me because they thought I was adorable and could become well known in the area and possibly outside of it. That blew my mind to hear. I didn't think much of it until others were telling me similar things.

That night was one of the highlights of my life and I continued to try and get better each time. I would go to more open mics. There were a few open mics in a row where some of my material was falling flat and the crowd wasn't laughing. I started to record all my sets and play them back to see how it sounded from a casual point of view. I'd share it with friends and they were hesitant to give feedback because they wanted to tell me everything was good and didn't want to hurt my feelings. I told them they needed to be honest with me because I would never get better if I don't know why something didn't work. Sometimes it seemed that I was trying too hard to be edgy or push the envelope when really I wasn't trying at all. I just said things that got people talking. Sometimes I said something that was too much to handle and could cross a line. So I had to learn where to tune some things down a bit and not to just try to say things to get a reaction in hopes of shocking someone. It was a rough adjustment but one I was willing to make to try to stay diverse and different from everyone else.

I ended up getting booked as a regular at this one club. I did an open mic there and the owner came up to me after and told me he wanted me. I also didn't know that he meant he wanted me sexually as well. He offered me a recurring gig and I was the host for one of the shows and that was my first time hosting. I also ended up getting an enemy who spread some nasty rumors about me. The club owner also still wanted to suck my dick in the worst way. He was very attractive and he was older in his mid forties and in good shape. His hair wasn't totally grey yet but was pretty close. I found him very attractive but I didn't want to do anything with him and then have rumors start to fly around. I didn't want to be known as a guy that only got gigs because I slept around. It was very hard to ignore his advances and for a few weeks I stopped being available. I just knew if I kept going week after week that something would happen and word would somehow get around. There were already a few people speculating that I might have something going on with him. I thought spending a few weeks away would put those rumors to rest. Little did I know more rumors would start.

He ended up partnering with a new entertainment director to get a variety of acts into the club, as comedy itself wasn't cutting it. Only the woman he hired had no idea what the hell she was doing. He still would get me booked on shows and had a lot of say in getting me there. This entertainment director didn't seem as impressed. She wanted to phase out comedy and get live music. Only she had no grasp of what good music or what people wanted to hear was. She would book bands that weren't getting booked anywhere else. They weren't getting booked elsewhere because they had bad attitudes, weren't reliable, or just sucked that much. She started doing the same thing for comedians. She booked this one guy and I can't remember his name to tell you the truth, but he had made it a bit. He claims he was a headliner in some bigger areas, and even appeared on some tv show. Both of which I think were lies, because he just seemed like a liar the moment I met him. He told these outlandish stories of all these things he did. Things that just didn't seem possible for a guy that was that fat. Like you really ran a 25 mile marathon last year and came in second place? Did you gain 200 pounds in one year?

For some reason he disliked me and would talk about me. He trashed me in his act and he trashed me behind the scenes. Things he said in the act were borderline roast material but things he said behind the scenes were just unnecessary and uncalled for. He would try to tell other people that I wasn't dependable, or I would trash talk other people so I would get booked on a show instead of them. Those were minimal compared to some of the other things. He told people I would suck their dicks if I could have their spot on the show. He one time told people I'd suck them off in the parking lot if they came to the show or I'd pay their door fee just so I was "drawing" an audience. He seemed rather obsessed with me sucking dick. Maybe because I would never suck his? I tried to not let it bother me and just continue working on me. I wanted to be the bigger person even though he was ten times my size.

We rarely got booked on the same show so I never had to see him much. Then the unthinkable happened. We were booked on this big show that would feature music and comedy and I was given the headlining spot and he wasn't much like he was expected. He threw a huge tempter tantrum and bitched to anyone that would listen. Although I think the owner was really trying to butter up to me so I would finally hook up with him. The guy who trash talked me was not too thrilled but I didn't care I had the headlining act and he didn't. I worked hard for this spot so I didn't care what rumors he spread at this point. This show sounded good on paper but when it came time to the actual show it was a hot mess from the start.

It wasn't laid out in a logical way at all. Bands would play and then comedians would perform in between and there were two stages. The problem with this is most of the audience was there to see the bands and the comedians got ignored. The audience would be loud and talk over the comedians, or the bands would be doing a sound check and it would over power the comedians. The guy who talked shit about me failed to show up. He spent all that time talking about me and how unreliable I was and that I frequently no showed and here he flat out no showed without even contacting anyone. It was glorious and a small victory for me.

I remember it came time for my part and I instantly did what I could to get anyone to pay attention to me. I remember when I did my intro bit I took general command of the room from the start. They barely clapped but I was like "Oh hell no we are doing this again" So I walked off stage and walked back on and redid my intro and said "now you motherfucker's need to make some noise, get as loud as you can I wanna hear you scream because shit is going down!" For some reason that seemed to get people pumped. I guess I carried myself with this rock star vibe. Someone at one of the tables was talking very loud and I wasn't having that. I went over to the table with the mic and started having a conversation with them. I just remember telling the audience I saw him at the gay club last week and that I sucked his dick in the bathroom. He seemed so offended and it was wonderful because the crowd started to pay attention and was laughing. He was denying it and I was like "don't worry I'll do the same thing I did last week, "Hey bartender bring this man a double shot of Jack." He was embarrassed and shut up quickly, although I did really buy him a double shot of Jack because I am a man of my word. I remember saying "Hey while I am here does anyone else want some shots on me?" Cheers from the crowd! "Oh I can't suck all your dicks but if you still want shots on me I'll lay on the stage and you can all do a circle jerk on me." The crowd was just eating it up because I was so out there and being outrageous. None of my set called for any of that but it was working. When I got back on the stage the audience was hanging on my every word. Even the band the band that was setting up on the other stage just stood there watching me.

Someone towards the end of my set was a bit too drunk and tried to heckle me but I put him in his place really quick. I don't remember what I said but it was a good burn that the audience cheered at and ate up. I ended my set on a high note and introduced the final band of the night. My night was a success in every way. It was hard to believe just how much I accomplished in a few months. I wasn't even doing comedy for a full year.  I was maybe eight months into it. Just to have so much happen so fast was just phenomenal. I was a young guy in my early twenties and felt like I was on top of the world. The entertainment booker tried to not pay me but I made sure I got my money. The club owner came up to me and offered to give me a massage in his office. I let him rub my shoulders a bit and teased him a bit but I wasn't going to let him do anything sexual with me.

I got home and some crazy shit went down both from the show side and my personal life. The owner had received an angry letter because some woman in the audience was offended by my set and said she would never be back. He liked and wanted me too much to not allow me to come back so basically told her to fuck off. I guess I was doing my job right because nobody paid attention to the comedians all night. The guy from one of the bands reviewed the show and thought that I was the highlight of the show and the only memorable comedian. He said I could go far and should pack up my bags and grab that brass ring and I was better than the stuck up people in this area. That meant a lot to me to hear I was so well reviewed. Truth be told a lot of the comedians all had amazing sets that night. The problem was nobody was listening and to them it was just another show and an easy payday for them. They were content. For me it was a big headlining gig and I wanted to treat it as such. I got home to a message from a certain someone who wanted to come back into my life. This is what I was talking about a bit earlier.

This guy's name was James. He was the definition of a Latin sweetheart. It hadn't even been a little over a year since we had dated. At the time that we dated. I had just turned twenty and he had just turned nineteen the month before. He was having some issues with his current boyfriend. His boyfriend was actually this guy that I used to go to school with back in the day. His boyfriend was super gay and really too into himself. The bleached teeth with the orange spray tan and the over gelled hair and the clothes he couldn't afford with a sparkly phone case. He had dropped off James at my house one time and this guy was not happy that James was staying with me. He threatened me that if we did anything he would come kick my ass. I would have loved to have seen him try to be honest with you. That could be a comedy skit right there. Then I listened to him belittle James in my driveway. He was yelling at him for wearing the wrong clothes and that he looked like trash. All of this just verbal abusive garbage.

I don't know how we came to even be friends. I think he was going through his boyfriend's friends list and for some reason I was on his friends list. He hit me up on a private message and introduced himself. I had seen them around together a few times so I knew he was attractive and a little bit about him. I let him stay a few days at my place and we just developed a close friendship that soon turned into a relationship. I was falling for him fast. He had this hold on me and I don't know what it

was but there was something about him. He listened
to me talk about my feelings, I felt sympathy for his
situation, he was gentle, kind, caring. Just a lot of
what I look for in a guy and he seemed interested in
me. He stayed with me for two months and over
that time we built what I thought was an
unbreakable bond. Then he started acting strange.
Little did I know that this was just a thing that he
did. He leads guys on so they feel bad for him and
then when you get too close he shuts the door and
moves onto someone else that could either spoil him
or just be taken control of by him. It works because
most people he met fell for him. The one's who saw
through the bullshit were usually on his trash talk
list. I was just blinded by the idea of finding my
prince charming. I was a fucking idiot.

He ran away and didn't come back over for a
few days. I had no idea where he was. He was
logged into my computer and he had cleared most
of his message history. He didn't want me to know
that he was going somewhere else. I didn't log him
out of the computer simply on accident because I
was running late for work. He showed up at my
workplace with a break up letter. He said he had
found somewhere else to stay but appreciates all I
did for him but right now he isn't looking for a long

term relationship. I was a bit crushed but took it in
stride. I got home from work and didn't realize he
was still logged into my computer and he had a ton
of messages from this guy named Tony. Tony was
near thirty five and quite a downgrade from me. He
more resembled the really gay guy from right before
me, but an older version. I just read these messages
about how he was going to buy him all this stuff,
and that James should dump me and Tony would
give him better sex. James and I weren't even having
sex because I knew he was with the town's biggest
slut right before me. I just was paranoid of catching
and STD so I with held for the most part. We were
intimate but hardly sexual. Tony went on to talk
about some of the things in the previous messages. I
couldn't pretend to be James because it would have
been too obvious if I was like... "I'm sorry I forgot
what I messaged you, what are we doing again?".
Luckily, Tony was filling in a big portion of the
blanks and I could read between the lines. He
wanted to go have sex with this guy, was done
using me for a place to stay, and was now moving
onto this guy. I felt cheated but not in relationship
terms. More of I was cheated on a chance to say
goodbye and say what I wanted to say to him.

Now we fast forward to shortly after a year later after the comedy show. I was getting closer to twenty-two but I wasn't there yet. James had messaged me and said that he wanted to talk to me. He apologized for the way he acted and he had been wanting to talk to me for a while but was too afraid that I was bitter. I decided to give him a chance to talk and I tried to keep my guard up the best I could. I agreed to meet him for coffee. When we met for coffee, I was acting tough. I was acting as if shit didn't phase me and I was trying to sound a lot more mature than I was. I really wanted to show off and make it appear that he wouldn't be able to manipulate me again. I wanted to be the better man and I also wanted to tell him off, but I also wanted to have another try in case he was somehow a different person.

He had been dating yet another horrible guy this time the guy's name was Ted. Ted was cheating on him left and right and was never home and they had been renting a house together. He cried to me and I just fell into his head games yet again. I agreed to go back to his place with him to keep him company. Things escalated quickly. We snuggled up and clothes were coming off. We ended up kissing and touching each other all over until we took turns fucking each other. We fell asleep after and the next morning I woke up and we were snuggled and happy. Things felt good, things felt right. It didn't feel like he cheated on his boyfriend when he pretty much did. I had to get going because I had work and his boyfriend was actually coming home.

Over the next few weeks we would hang out and go on these dates and be somewhat intimate. He would send me flirty texts or pics of himself. We would get together and we would have sex a few more times. He was leading me on again but I just wasn't picking up on it. We were on a very romantic date on a pier and we were snuggling on the dock having a picnic. I asked him about his relationship and that I could treat him better. He didn't say much and seemed slightly put off but kissed me.

I'm not quite sure what happened but a few days later I get this nasty text message from him and that he doesn't want to see me anymore. He said things had never been better between him and his boyfriend. Um, What the fuck? I was so pissed off but I figured this was never going to happen. A few days passes and I actually end up seeing him in a coffee shop. I was with friends and he was with his sister. He had nowhere to run and nowhere to hide. I approached him and thanked him for wasting my time, and that he was the biggest piece of shit I had ever met in my entire life.

His sister got offended and started arguing with me. I wasn't about to play this game, so I told her that none of this concerned her. She then was like, "My brother ain't like you, yo shirt that too damn small." I guess she was trying to call me fat. I wore tight fitting clothing because I had a pretty nice body and I wanted to show it off. I then said to her. "If your brother didn't want anything to do with me like you claim, he wouldn't constantly be sending me nude pics of himself and asking me to fuck him! Now would he?" She just jumps back "bullshit he don't send you no nudes I wanna see." I said to her, "You want to see your brother naked? No wonder your family is so fucked up?". She kept trying to say shit to me but I said to her, "Look you nasty as puta skank. This ain't about you, you can get all up in my face. Snap your fingers in a z formation and claw me with your std infected nails. So go ahead and punch me and make my day. The cops are at the gas station next door. They'd be here in a matter of seconds to arrest your ass. Since you already have a record for drug possession and a few unpaid tickets. Your brother don't even like you. He talks shit about you constantly so go for it protect the little asshole, don't believe me I got video and voicemails of that too."

She slowly shut up and walked outside and I guess she was going to try to run into the building with her car. I am not sure she got in the car and started revving the engine up. Before James, could utter a word I gave my final words.

"Now you have nowhere to run, you have an angry sister. You aren't cheating me out of a goodbye this time and you sure in hell are not getting away with out me telling you what a disgusting piece of shit you are. Goodbye, James! I hope you one day stop acting like a spoiled brat and become a good man. Until that day comes don't even try to talk to me again. Now goodbye you fucking loser."

There was something so damn freeing about finally being able to speak my mind and get in the last word. All I wanted previously was an explanation and I never got one. This time I was the one that was in control. I thought I was done with crazy people for a while but then my one female friends  was trying to get a romantic thing going with me. She's really not worth mentioning by name, so I'm going to call her Jane. Jane had this reddish brown hair and it was quite long, and flat. Very pale skinned much like myself but she might have been a few shades lighter. She usually caked on her makeup and it looked awful. She was twenty but her makeup sometimes made her look near thirty. I hated that makeup!

We had some mutual friends and I remember one time we kissed during a game of truth or dare. I think from that moment she had a bit of a crush on me and I found her personality charming. There was a point in time where we just hung out nearly everyday. Some of our best moments would just be driving around town in my shitty car and listening to music and talking about life. I would talk to her about my crazy dating life and she would listen and give her opinion. I once dated this crazy guy named Matt. All of my friends liked him, but there was something that I found odd about him. It made me uncomfortable. She told me I should trust my instincts on it and she was right. He was on several different medications. Mostly it was stuff to stop hallucinations or various voices in his head. He would be reckless and out of control if he missed too many doses. Not something I wanted to get involved with. He was fine as long as he stayed on

the medication but I just wasn't comfortable with the
risk.

Our dynamic started to change and she was
acting jealous over every little thing. She wanted to
control all aspects of my life. She gave me a list of
people one day that I wasn't allowed to talk to. She
said she did it for all of her friends. There was more
to the story than I realized. Her mother was friends
with this one woman I knew from the bar I went to
karaoke at. Her mother also visited the bar. One of
the people on Jane's do not hang out with list was
karaoke woman's son. Karaoke woman and Jane's
mother used to be good friends but had a falling out.
Jane dated karaoke woman's son for a bit of time
and he was one of the people on the do not hang out
list. Karaoke woman was also off limits but I
couldn't really control if she would talk to me at
karaoke.

It turned out that Jane was quite pissed off at
me for this and yelled at me one night over the
entire thing. We had our little argument and went
our separate ways. One random time I go to karaoke
I hear whispers and people are talking about me as I
walk in the door. Some of the straight guys are
giving me high fives and offering to by me drinks. I
feel like a rock star but I am not sure why. Evidently

Jane's mother told everyone in the bar that I had sex with the older karaoke woman in the bar's bathroom. It was supposed to be a rumor that was meant to destroy us both but it just made me seem cool. I didn't feel cool and I didn't want people thinking it was true but it also didn't ruin my image. I later found out through some other friends that Jane had come up with the whole thing as a way to ruin my friendship with karaoke woman. Jane told her mother what to say to everybody in the bar. Her mother was even bragging about it after getting piss ass drunk and trying to pick up whatever biker looking guy she could get.

I was furious, mostly because this is someone I considered a close friend and she was trying to manipulate my friendship to her advantage. I also was seriously considering dating her. Making her the first woman that I would have dated in years. The problem was a lot of the people that I socialized with also were friends with her. Although they were on the approved hang out list. I didn't know that she had told a few of those people about the bar incident. She of course twisted to it where she was playing the victim and that I made her mother cry because I said her mother was the one who hooked up in the bathroom. Then she started telling them that her ex boyfriend was an abuser and threw her down the stairs. That was not a true statement either. She had been notorious for telling lies so people would feel sorry for her. A lot of times it worked because she was so convincing.

I'd like to say that is where things came to an end but the drama just continued with her. When she told those mutual friends about the bar incident she made it seem like I was the bad guy and that I should apologize to her. There was a new person to our group. It was this big lesbian chick. She was the very definition of a bull dyke. I mean that in the nicest way possible..... of course. She wasn't familiar with her games. I didn't know that she was hanging out with Jane that night. She and Jane were at this diner with the usual circle of friends. So, Bull invited me out and had told me it was only her and two or three other people from the circle. People that I didn't have any issues with. I thought something was up but I was hungry and wanted food so I decided to go out anyway. To my surprise when I arrived at the diner, Jane was sitting there. I said my hellos to everyone and then saw, Jane and excused myself from the group. I said, "I'm sorry guys I'm not going to stay, I was called to work, (I really was called to work but was planning on eating before hand, they didn't know I wasn't starting for another two hours.) and I have to be there in a little bit. Right now is also not a good time. I'm having some issues with Jane, and sorry Jane I didn't know you would be here tonight but now is not the time to discuss anything, and I don't want to bring anyone else into it. So I hope you all have a good night."

I was pissed because it was an obvious set up and I just don't know how I didn't see it coming. I had my suspicions but I didn't think she would be that petty or manipulative after all the previous drama. As I was turning around to leave I hear Jane screaming, "What do you mean you have a fucking problem with me!" What the fuck did I do!" I love how she was acting as if she had know idea of the bar situation and all the other lies she had been caught I. "Jane, we'll talk another time. You know what happened with the bar. Your mother told practically the whole bar. I'm upset right now and I just need time to myself for a bit. I don't want to do this here." She jumped back with, "Oh we are gonna do this here!" She started yelling and shouting and making a huge scene as I was leaving the diner. I did my best to ignore her and just walked as fast I could to my car. One of the waitresses had stopped her on the way out because they thought she was trying to bail on her bill. That bought me the extra few seconds I needed. However it didn't buy me enough time to leave the parking lot. The next thing you know she is banging on my window and trying to break my glass with her boot. She takes off her boots and she jumps onto the hood of my car. She screams and hisses at me, "I dare you to drive off!". I wanted to so badly but I did not. Finally, Bull comes out. Evidently she felt bad about setting everything up so she came out to get, Jane off my car. She picked up Jane and carried her over her shoulder and Jane was kicking and screaming and then she spit at my car. I was able to finally back out and I see, Bull still just carrying Jane in the rear view mirror.

After that I vowed to never talk to Jane again. I had been working on some music around the same time. I was doing an open mic or something like it. I was partnering up with a friend who could play guitar. I wrote a song about an abusive relationship and being tired of drama that comes with it. Completely unrelated to Jane, but little did I know she was at the lounge where the open mic was going on that night and heard the song. She thought I was talking about her, so when I got home I got an endless amount of threatening and angry messages from her. She chose not to confront me at the open mic for some reason or another. I was thankful she didn't because she was quite good at making a scene. I couldn't deal with that kind of drama anymore. I texted her back and told her I couldn't be friends with her anymore and to just leave me alone. I was also changing my number right after sending that text. I wasn't giving it to any of our shared friends. To be honest with you I cut off communication with most people in that circle. I was tired of dealing with bullshit. I had other things I wanted to focus on and I felt like a lot of them were just holding me back, as well as being terrible influences. Not people I wanted to associate myself with. I was ready for something different.

# CHAPTER 12 – Paying my dues

Comedy was going really well for me but I honestly was just getting burned out. I stopped performing at the one club that I was becoming a regular at because the new entertainment director had no idea what she was doing. Evidently the owner was in the process of selling her the club and she wanted more music and less comedy because she saw no money to be made in comedy. She wasn't entirely wrong. I was still doing shows on a regular basis but it was really hard to keep pushing and drive two to three hours to just get a few minute sets in. Plus I really needed some fresh material. I got into doing a lot of what had worked because I was just too lazy to write new material. Anyone who had seen me before would have heard all of these jokes. I didn't want to be that comedian who did that kind of thing. I wanted to keep it fresh. I decided I needed to just take a break. Somehow during that break wrestling was calling my name!

I wanted to put everything with the previous couple years behind me and this felt like the new start I was looking for. I think I responded to an ad that was placed on a local online classified. It was a new wrestling school that was starting. I decided to send them an email and they got back to me almost right away. They were telling me all the information I would need. It was very similar to what I've seen before. I would be having a tryout and if I passed the tryout or did well on the tryout I can move onto training. Although since you are giving them money I can't see how anyone really fails the tryout. I mean maybe if they didn't want to do the training after seeing how intense it is. I acted like I was a total newbie to this all and that it was my first time. It had been years at this point since I did anything in a ring. I was doing some wrestling matches on the side with some friends and that but that was nothing intense. So it actually felt like in a lot of ways that I was new to this.

I was given the address to the tryout and it was in the middle of freakin nowhere in someone's back yard. I was like please tell me this isn't some sort of backyard wrestling thing. I mean I did that in my day as well but I had previous training to where I felt like I could safely do things. I had checked this company and they had an upcoming show and some of the names checked out and lined up with local indy performers. I was told that it was only a temporary thing and that they are working on getting a building. They have a ring with a steel frame, they are just finalizing the lease with this one building manger at this old warehouse. The warehouse was creepy but I will get to that in a few moments.

I introduced myself and shook everyone's hands. The one trainer was already impressed that I seemed to know the proper protocol. The tryout was as I expected it would be. Learning a few of the basic bumps, learning lockups, and doing some push ups, squats and sit ups. I enjoyed it so I decided I would come back and train a bit more. There were three trainers in total. One his name was Dave and he was a bigger guy but let me tell you he could move in the ring. He was the head trainer and he trained the other two trainers. He had many years of experience and ran his own training school for a long time, but the owner of the building had sold the property. Which seems like it is a rather common occurrence anytime you are renting a building. You just never know what the owner will do.

Dave saw a lot of potential in me right from the start and pulled me aside to tell me a few things. First he suggested I take a warm bath when I get home and invest in icy hot because my body is gonna be sore. Then he told me he that a lot of guys come in here and instantly have no respect, are cocky, and don't listen and end up being a problem.

185

He told me as long as I continue to be respectful to people, keep my mouth shut and listen I will do well. There were times I was thinking in my head. "Dude I already did this and it looked fine, why the hell am I doing it again?" I didn't want to say that because I knew I wasn't the trainer and I didn't have close to twenty years in the business. So my thoughts wouldn't much matter anyway.

The other two trainers I can't remember if they were brothers or best friends but they wrestled as a tag team.  Their names were Adam and Sam. They were younger guys around twenty-eight and thirty, but they had been wrestling for a few years. As trainers they were nowhere near Dave's level. Dave was the one who mostly took command and they just took orders or really would turn to Dave if they didn't know what to do as far as instruction.

I kept coming back for the next few weeks. Training was two days a week and each week I learned more and got better. I was progressing faster than a lot of people do and I constantly listened to any criticism to see what I could do better. One of the issues I had early on was getting in my own head. I would overthink a lot of things and that is not something you want to be doing in a match. It comes to that point where if you overthink

something you could hurt the other person and you
don't want to do that. In some cases it was hard for
me to overcome that but when I did my
performance would instantly get better. I think my
advice in that situation is just take a deep breath and
just go for it. Stop thinking about what can go
wrong and dive head first. Instinct will take over
and if your brain tells you to protect yourself you
will. You will naturally know what to do because
that is just what your instincts are for.

Throughout my training I would be "paying
my dues" doing a lot of the work that nobody
wanted to be doing but earning the respect of other
wrestlers in the process. I'd play whatever role
needed to be filled at a show. One show it might be
security, another it might just be bell ringer or ring
crew. I always stayed to clean up and help out
anyway I could. A lot of the promotions in my area
shared the same wrestlers. So even though I wasn't
training with that promotion if my trainers were
booked on the show. Chances are I was there and
had some role in making the show work.

Funny story is one time there was this tag
team match and it was going over time. The
wrestler's were given very specific instructions on
what to do and when to end the match. My head

trainer was running this show and he was peaking through the curtain to signal the ref to end the match. The ref passed on the message to all involved in the tag team match but they didn't listen to a word he said and continued to go on. I was the bell ringer for this show and Dave yells at me "Ring the damn bell!" I start ringing the bell and everyone in the crowd is staring at me, the wrestlers in the ring stop what they are doing and stare at me. I run over to the announcer and tell him "Dave stopped the match for going over time. This has become a no contest." The announcer makes the announcement and the crowd instantly boos. I don't think they realize that Dave was the one who made the decision. One of the heel wrestlers tells me to "Fuck off" in character of course and the crowd eats it up and starts chanting, "FUCK THE TIME KEEPER". I walk back to my area where the bell is and the crowd is booing me a long the way. I just play it off like I don't give a shit and eat up the boos. I give a "whatever" motion a "talk to the hand" motion to the crowd and the wrestlers in the ring. I get back to my station and Dave peaks his head out and says, "That was awesome, I just tested you, and you got yourself some heat. I wasn't sure how you would handle that but I'm impressed." I loved the thrill of that night and that made me want to do this even more. I had people coming up to me after the show and being upset that I ended that match, some even were calling it a "screwjob" which I took as a huge compliment.

My training continued and the new building opened and I was no longer training in the wooden ring in the backyard. It was nice to be in the ring that we were going to be using. The building was an old warehouse that was turned into a carpet store. We were upstairs and the carpet store was downstairs. It worked out well because the venue that the shows were at was right across the street. It was a performing arts center and it was a decent size. We could just move things across the street for the shows. It worked out quite nicely actually. The owner of the building was freaking strange though. He was really pushing on installing an open shower area in the corner of the one building and he frequently came up to watch training. He just wanted to make sure everyone was clean and wouldn't mind paying for an open shower area. It actually seemed like a really big project and like it would cost a lot of money. I think he just wanted to watch people shower to be honest with you. He kept talking about how the shower area could reduce the rent. I think it was like you won't pay as much in rent if you let me watch you shower. Something just seemed really strange to me about that.

A few months had passed by and Dave asks me if I want to be in a match. I was so nervous but I of course jumped at it. I found out it would be a tag team match and he wanted to come up with something that would be different and help introduce me to the audience. All he knew is that he wanted it to be an underdog type of thing. Over the course of a few shows, about three or four. Which shows at this point were every two weeks one wrestler would get double teamed by this tag team. They'd pick on him and bully him and I'd be the guy that teams up with him as a rookie and we'd get the underdog win. We were bouncing ideas back and forth and I joking said something about "What if I'm just like this dorky concession stand boy selling hot dogs and the guy getting beat up is my best friend, and I'm sick of watching it from the sidelines." I don't know what made me think of that idea but I thought for sure he would think it was the dumbest thing ever.

"You know what? That's kind of stupid, but there is something there that might actually be able to work. We're looking for an under dog scenario.

People in the crowd might laugh at the idea and think you are both a joke. Although if you both work well together you could potentially win them over. It's a risky move, it needs some tweaking but I think we can make it work." Dave said to me.

I was shocked that he took my idea seriously. We worked on the idea during training. How the gimmick would come to be and how we would work it in so it wouldn't be completely random. We decided I would come out to "the fast food song" and my gear would be colorful like a fast food uniform. My boots were red and I had these long blue tights and a red vest and a blue visor. I took inspiration from the song's music video. We would drop hints over the weeks that it was coming. The heel tag team would pick on my tag team partner and then say something harassing in my direction. Like "Hey hot dog boy, get your ass over here and bring us some food.... Hurry the fuck up my grandma moves faster than this." When I'd bring the food they'd shove it my tag team partner's face  and then poor the drink over my head. We would set it up so I didn't look like a wrestler and wouldn't take a bump but would help my partner out of the ring.

We tried a few things like that for a couple of weeks. Just stuff that would get sympathy for my partner. One week it was his "birthday" and they had ordered a cake that was being held at the concession stand. I delivered it to the ring placed it on the table and when I had my back turned they'd shove me out of the way. Of course they then picked up the cake a shoved his face in it.

We were getting closer to the match so my partner was coming to the training to help me get match ready. I wasn't going to have any huge part of the match. I'd basically get the "hot tag" and do a few drop kicks and some quick moves and take a bump or two but nothing too involved. I mean I was still in training and didn't much know everything I needed to know about working a match.

My partner was a cool guy. He was in his late twenties and had only been wrestling for about two years. He was a smaller guy around five foot seven inches. He was a skinnier guy with longer hair but he could really move in the ring. He had a flashy ring name. It was something like Mark Cruise. I mean it was common sounding but it was a pun. He was a bit of a high flier and a lot of wrestling fans are called marks so it was pretty much a play on words. Our opponents had some typical heel name and they were bigger guys.

At training we did a run through of what the match was going to be like and how everything would play out and what I would say. I also needed a name because I didn't have one. Some people knew me as Aiden, so I had just added Franks to the end of it because my gimmick was selling hot dogs. It was stupid and clever enough at the same time.

It was the night of my debut and the worst thing was I couldn't spend all night just hiding in the back and waiting for my match. I actually had to work the concession stand as part of my gimmick and because it was what I was doing to "pay my dues". I had these boot covers over my wrestling boots so I wouldn't damage them or get them covered in grease, or so nobody would notice. I had a pair of snap on pants over my tights and had a regular button up shirt over my vest. When it came time for our segment I was terrified. I wasn't sure how the audience would respond or if my mind would just go blank.

So they have my partner come out to the ring as if he is about to do a singles match. The heel tag team comes out and starts picking on him like usual. Then they continue to do their normal skit where they have me bring them food but I refuse and grab the mic that was hidden behind the concession stand. I'm beyond nervous and I just am focusing on getting my words out. Trying to remember things I had from acting and speaking classes. I said something a long the lines of. "For the last few weeks, I've had to watch you humiliate and embarrass Mark. Instead of bringing you food I'm gonna bring you my boot to shove up your ass!" Some people in the crowd cheered and some laughed but at least there was a reaction and not the dreaded "What" chant. I challenged them to a tag team match and they laughed at me and accepted the challenge, joking about how easy it was going to be. Just playing up their villain roles perfectly and making the audience hate them even more but feel a bit more sympathy for us. My music hit and I made my way from behind the concession stand. I had taken my boot covers off right before the segment and ripped open my shirt and rip off pants to reveal my wrestling gear.

The walk through the audience to the ring seemed to take hours. In reality it was probably about a minute but I just was trying to soak everything in. People in the crowd were patting me on the back and wishing me luck. Some were still laughing and others were texting on their phones. I tried not to think of any of that and just focus on what I had to do. When I got to the ring I stood face to face the heel tag team with my partner by my side. We did a double drop kick to knock them both down and then continued to do some kicks. The referee came over to back us off of them and when they got up they charged at us pushing the referee out of the way. They gave us a cheap shot and then I got to take my first bump of the night. They did these double vertical suplexes. The referee comes back and separates them for us and pushes us into separate corners. The bell then rings and my partner is in the match first.

I'm trying to just absorb everything and watch the match at the same time. Trying to scan the faces of people in the crowd as well as keeping my self together. I don't want to let anyone see how incredibly nervous I am. It comes to the part of the match where they collide into one another and knock each other down. They are both crawling for the hot tag and I now have to get in the zone. The heel team gets the tag first and then my partner. I jump into the ring and go to deliver my first drop kick to the other guy. Then his partner starts to get up using the ropes and I deliver a drop kick to him which knocks him out of the ring. I turn around to get an Irish whip into the corner. I tried to hit the corner as hard as I could and make sure I was selling everything. He comes charging at me but I dodge the attack and as he bounces off the corner I roll him up into a two count. We both get up and do a chain of moves with a little bit of back and forth. I've been in the ring for a few minutes and I whip my opponent into our corner and tag my partner in. He comes in and we deliver a double suplex. He goes for the pin as I am exiting the ring but our opponent's tag team partner comes into make the save. I jump back in the ring to brawl with him and the referee is trying to separate us. We roll out of the ring and continue our fight outside the ring. Meanwhile my partner was hit with a low blow and a roll up but he kicks out. The heel starts arguing with the referee that it should have been a three count. I didn't see the move my partner did to get him laying in the center of the ring but the next thing you know I see my partner on the top rope doing a frog splash. I take a pulled punch which "knocks me" into some members of the audience and his tag team partner tries to break up the three count but doesn't get there in time. We won the match and my partner rolls out of the ring and comes over to me and we celebrate our first victory together. The crowd is loving it.

I can't begin to describe everything I was feeling. I was on such a high from that experience. This felt like something that I was born to do. I loved it and I wanted to do it more and get even better at it. I returned to training so I could prep for my debut solo match. My tag team partner ended up quitting the wrestling business shortly after that match. He had enjoyed wrestling but he felt that he had done everything he had wanted to do. He was fun to work with but in a way I was thrilled that I wouldn't have to keep being in a tag team with him. It was nothing against him, it was just that I felt being in a tag team would hold me back. It would be beneficial for me to be in the tag team while I was learning and getting better. I know in a lot of ways that is just how the business works. I just felt like I was destined for better things.

To get a bit more ring experience I was given the role of being tossed out of a battle royal. I didn't much yet have a gimmick so I still went by, Aiden Franks but I think I dropped the S because the fast food gimmick was no more. My gear was a lot more basic and less flashy. I think I opted for some red and black as my colors of choice. Just basic boots, trunks, elbow pads, knee pads, wrist tape and finger less gloves. I was going to be in the ring all of about five minutes max. I came out to a remix of Promise This by Cheryl Cole. I loved that song at the time and even though I didn't have a character I felt the fast tempo of the song worked for me. I didn't try to do anything too flashy. This was a fifteen man battle royal and I wasn't quite skilled enough to take any dumb risks. I kept everything to a minimal. My main focus was making sure I didn't hurt myself when I got tossed over the top rope. I had practiced going over the top rope a few times in training but part of it terrified me. Thankfully when it came time for me to get eliminated I was able to clear my head and go over the rope. I didn't much think of how my landing looked because nobody knew who I was and I'm sure they weren't watching too closely. I went up and over and took my bump to the floor without injury.

Over the next few weeks I'd be working towards the goal of my solo match. I tried to get as much of paying my dues as possible. The problem was a lot of the promotions in my area weren't doing shows because of drama. I'm not going to The one that I helped out a few times at had a problem with the venue starting to charge more for renting the community center. The promoter had an issue and ended up blasting the community center on social media and that became the end of all shows there. As far as I know they did not relocate to another venue and that was the end of that promotion. People had egos and it got in the way of doing business. Unfortunately it just wasn't good if you were trying to make a name for yourself.

One of the other big promotions in my area and one that I wasn't interested in doing anything with was known for bringing in wrestlers that had once made it big. While I respected that these guys worked their asses off to get where they were, I just felt it hurt the little guy like me. A lot of them had booking prices of anywhere from $800-$2000. Not being a promoter myself I can't speak on if there is money to be made there. It was just something that felt like another obstacle to overcome. Not to upstage the star studded performer, but to even get people to be interested in me when a star of that caliber is there.

Back to what I was saying here. I just wanted to work on shows but I knew that I still had to go through some things before I was even at that level. I was able to start working solo matches but not without having some guidance first. It would be a while before I was able to go on my own completely without having to go to training weekly.

When the time came for my first solo match it was with one of my trainers. That was going to be nice because they could carry me through the match if I fucked up. I still didn't have a gimmick exactly. There was more planning put into my debut tag match than there was my solo match. We were both faces so this was basically just a trainer vs student type of thing. I also didn't want to be associated with my fast food gimmick from previously. I wasn't ashamed of it in anyway. I was lucky that I had as much input as I did and that they allowed me to have that creative freedom with it. Normally in a lot of these situations you are just thrown into something and you have to work with it. You don't get a choice. You do what the guy in charge tells you to do. I just wanted to start developing a character organically. I wanted to ability to do the talking and then build the character from there. My head trainer was throwing some gimmick ideas around but he wanted to get my first match out of the way to make sure that I could even cut it in the ring as a solo performer. Why waste all that time if I wasn't even ready?

The thing that sucked was having to lose my first solo match. My trainer also had a finisher that I had to run into. It had to be fluid and smooth and I had to sell the hell out of it. Luckily I was always a natural at selling. I guess years of acting in theatre paid off. I took the finisher had the ref do the three count and then my trainer helped me up to shake my hand and congratulate me and raise my hand. I suppose the loss was to help make me look like a gutsy performer. Might make the crowd get sympathy for me and be like, "Wow he tried his best and is out here living his dream." I'm not quite sure if that was the reasoning but for me it sounded good.

I would go back and resume training for a bit before I would hit an issue. I wanted to keep training and I got so far along but life outside of wrestling was starting to get in the way. I started school and I was going for my degree in digital media. I was working a lot outside of wrestling to help pay for school, and I had met someone prior to my training and it was what would become my first long term relationship. I decided that I was going to put my training on hold because I had hit my first goal. I wrestled my first live match and while it felt incredible, I was ok waiting a bit to do another one. I wanted to be serious about school and work and as much as I loved wrestling it was becoming a distraction.

# CHAPTER 13 – Let's get sexy

A little before my training I ended up meeting someone that I started to fall hard for. I messaged him on a dating site and did not think that for a second he would entertain the idea of going out with me. His name was Stephen. He was just starting out doing some photo shoots and was hoping to become a model and an actor. He was one of the most attractive guys that I ever dated. He was the same age as me and had this playful wavy brown hair and greenish brown eyes.

Our first date we kept things simple and just went out to this little pizza place that he lived near. We talked about comic books, movies, tv shows, and music we liked. It was wonderful because we shared a lot of similar interests and this date was just going well. He ended up asking me to stay over which is not something that I originally had planned.

That night was of course one of the most magical I have ever experienced with a guy. I can't quite pinpoint what made it so special but something felt real and as if I were missing that. We somehow ended up having sex and it was the most incredible sex I had ever had in my life. It was raw and real and just everything I was looking for. We went on a few dates after that weekend and soon enough ended up being in a relationship.

Like I mentioned he was starting to get into doing acting type things and photo shoots. He didn't drive due to a medical condition. He had a form of epilepsy and his seizures had no rhyme or reason. Sometimes he could go weeks or months without having one and other times he'd have one weekly. The first one I ever witnessed was just a terrible experience. I had a friend who had a roommate who had seizures and I remember from dealing with her how to manage them. I at least was prepared and knew what to do in the event it happened.

We were watching one of the Fast and Furious movies and I fell asleep. He was on the computer and I awaken to the sound of him convulsing. I ran over to the chair and just kept an eye on everything and looked at the clock. I knew from doing some research in my free time that seizures over five minutes could be dangerous. His seizure was just under five minutes but after wards he did this new thing. At least he said it was new when I told him about it. He started walking around the house and he was in a zombie like state. He went to turn on the oven and then went to the bathroom to reach his hand in the toilet for no apparent reason. It was the strangest thing but it was some sort of state of confusion he was in after. That was only a temporary thing and he had not done anything like that after another seizure. That was just one small part of our relationship. He still liked to do a lot of things and never let that get in his way.

We shared similar interests in that we wanted to both do modeling and film work. It was easier for him to get work because he was the more attractive one. I would get work but I had to work with what I was given. A lot of times it felt like I was competing because if I got a better gig I'd be more likely to brag. His extra work was slightly more impressive than mine. He managed to be a featured extra in a movie called Fun Sized and had a small part in a Gym Class Heroes music video. I didn't get any kind of Extra work until closer to the end of our relationship. I was part of a series called Exile The Family You Choose as a featured Extra. That was a lot of fun to do. One of my bucket list items was to be the victim in a horror movie. Well this was a series and horror based so it was close enough! The only other thing I got to do was a little later was a promotional commercial as a club goer for this failed bar and club event finder type app.

At one point he started to do web cam modeling which I knew very little about. It was basically a thing where guys would buy credits to watch you jack off. I mean I don't know how else to put it. He asked me if I would want to do it with him. I was open to the idea and before you knew it I was being set up through his producer. I thought it was odd that he had someone overseeing him. Basically this producer type guy was more of a recruiter. I found out later that you could actually be your own boss and you'd keep more of what you make. This guy was just responsible for recruiting and making money off you. The more people he recruited that did well the more money he would make. He would make something like 20% and the site was already making like 60%. So then you'd be left with the other 20%. I'm not sure if those were the exact numbers but they weren't far off.

We didn't do it very long because he wanted to start focusing more on doing more modeling and more acting type projects and he thought that performing on web cam would hurt his chances. I'd say we maybe did it about a month together and there wasn't much money to be made. Truth be told in general the adult entertainment industry doesn't pay well unless you become a brand or well known.

Big named porn stars are going to of course make money because they worked their way up the ladder and had the right people behind them. No pun intended there although that fits! A lot of it from what I have seen  is young guys or ladies getting recruited and promised big things but of course not getting those big things in return. Like yeah there is potential to make lots of money but it isn't the get rich quick scheme that it looks like it is made out to be. I've met guys that claim to be porn producers and they say they can go to a bus station and a pay a cute looking twenty year old guy $50-$200 to do a video and they are more than willing because it's quick easy cash. Anyway these cam sites are similar to where the recruiters will make big promises. If you are going to get in camming then sign up directly with the site. This way you will at least make more money.

After he stopped doing it I tried my hand at going solo. I did manage to get my own fan base and that was nice but it was still just hard to make money. It wasn't something that was going to replace my regular job any time soon. Don't get me wrong there are people out there that did indeed make money. Basically they were the Twinks or Muscle Jocks, or Straight Guys. If you didn't fit into one of those categories than people generally weren't interested in you. If they were they were interested in what they could get for free.

I always felt I was aggressive in my approach and I took the time to learn what worked and what didn't work. I tried new room setups. New lighting techniques, upgrading my webcam. It just there is a lot of competition out there. That and I got tired of guys treating me the way they did. For every nice guy there was there was two more that were just nasty and vile. It just gets to you after a while. Being treated like you are worthless because you're attractive. It is a hard feeling to describe.

Since I was barely making any money doing it and I just couldn't stand to be treated like I was some sort of object that was always talked down to, I decided that the cam life wasn't for me.

Stephen and I would date for quite a while. I ended up being with him for a little over two years and we never officially broke up. He ended up moving out of state with this friend he knew. This friend wasn't at all crazy about me. He was a guy in his fifties and I stayed over there one weekend. We had a borderline awkward threesome and ever since then he just disliked me. Him living with a guy that didn't like me was going to make it a bit more difficult for us to do a long distance relationship. We just sort of drifted apart and I moved on to other things.

## CHAPTER 14 – Chyna was everything

I'm going to back track a little bit because I feel like this is the right time to talk about this. As a lot of you know Chyna was a huge influence on my life. I just remember watching her when I was younger and knowing that wrestling is something I wanted to do. The way she was portrayed just stuck with me. I felt an instant connection. Here is an outsider that is looked down upon for something and she's just kicking ass and not caring. Growing up I could relate to that. Feeling that I was different from other people and seeing someone I could relate to over coming that was a powerful thing.

I had met Chyna once before when I was younger and I was blown away but it was just in passing and it wasn't enough to really have a memorable experience. I found out that she was going to be doing an appearance at a local strip club. It was that phase of her career where she was just getting into porn. Myself at the time talking about and doing the very same thing with my boyfriend. I felt like I was starting to emulate her in some ways. I even considered my next move being trying to land some adult work before I hit my mid twenties. This woman previously influenced me to want to be a wrestler and now she was influencing me to want to

be an adult entertainer! Seriously though knowing
that I had the opportunity to potentially meet her
and thank her for the influence on my life I of course
had to jump on that.

I took my brother and my best friend out for a
guys night out. I knew they were both fans of Chyna
and I kept that as a surprise. They found it odd that I
wanted to go to a strip club but here I was pushing
for it hardcore. I swear I did not try to make that
sound dirty it is just that sometimes things I say just
sound that way. I had never really been to a straight
strip club before so I didn't know exactly what the
procedure was. I mean there was the one time in
Ireland where Nikki and I were going for "drink
specials with live entertainment" we just thought
the live entertainment was like some sort of band. A
band called Topless Naughty Girls. I mean it seemed
legit to me. How was I to know they literately meant
strippers. In Irealnd they played by some different
rules as far as Strip Clubs went so that was a whole
different game. The ladies weren't as leechy but they
were more aggressive. Like they fucking owned that
shit man! Anyway back to the point.

I sat up front because I wanted to get a good
seat for when Chyna performed. Meanwhile I had
ladies coming up to me and asking me to go to the

backroom to talk. I played dumb and pretended that I didn't know they were trying to sell my a private lap dance. From my days of working back in the gay club I knew that game. Granted we didn't sell private dances. In the gay world guys get the wrong idea and that leads to a lot of trouble. So anyway why would I pay $30 or $40 for a lap dance where someone can do whatever they want to me and if I accidentally make skin contact I get slapped. Yeah not really my cup of tea!

I threw a few ones out to some of the ladies that were performing and was more like get away from me money. They didn't hang around me because they knew I wasn't going to bring them any money. Then it came time for Chyna's bit. First they had the host introduce her and then she did this little bit where she "beats him up". That was entertaining and a throwback to her wrestling days. I think she delivered a DDT to him but well I mean it wasn't a big bump. He sort of fell into her and rolled over on the ground. Something they probably rehearsed a few times. They weren't in a ring they didn't really have to sell it. The crowd was there to see boobies!

I recall her doing three songs but I can't recall what they were. I loved it because she looked comfortable. It didn't look like it was something she was doing because of desperation. It looked like she was having the time of her life. She looked sexy, confident, and beautiful. I got so nervous when she crawled over to me and gave me a kiss on the cheek as I had my money in hand. She whispered in my ear "I'm running out of places to put it" in a sexy tone. She opened up her leg garter stocking and I put my five dollar bill in there. She gave me another kiss on the cheek, thanked me and headed to her next guy to get money from.

The last song she performed was the DX theme song. Which I thought was hilarious. Of course guys all over the bar were doing the DX CROSS CHOP and chanting "SUCK IT". I didn't know that she was doing a meet and greet after but when I found out she was I knew I had to get on that.

I remember going up to the area where the meet and greet was and I think it was her manager but I could be wrong. It could have been someone that worked at the venue. He was very rude and was like, "Chyna isn't ready yet, don't stand here" so I just stood on the opposite side and he didn't bark at me for standing there. When Chyna came out we decided to go to the end of the line because we felt we would have the most time with her at the end of the line. There wasn't a lot of people in line for the meet and greet. It was $20 and a lot of people had already blown their money on liquor, lap dances, or the strippers. There honestly couldn't have been more than twelve people in line. Which I know sounds like a depressing number, but this was also the earlier show. She still had two more apperances later in the evening. So the club wasn't quite as crowded as it could have been. This was the ten o'clock evening show. There was another one right before Midnight and then a later one before the club closed for the night.

Chyna was being super nice and respectful to everyone and giving them a few minutes each. She had a bit of time before the next showing. That guy from earlier was rushing some of the conversation but Chyna seemed to ignore him. I feel like she wanted to make sure that every fan there was getting the respect that they were giving her. That was one of the things that I always admired about her. She never seemed fake or anything like that. She put herself out there and sure she had her issues and demons but it seemed like she just wanted to be liked.

My friend and brother got to go before I did. I was the last person in line. My brother was talking about being in the fire service and Chyna tells the mean guy not to charge us for our photos. She said to my brother "I wouldn't feel right charging you guys knowing that you are in the fire service. It was people like you that when I was at my worst were there to save me." Those words stuck with me because you could see the pain on her face. You could see there was a time where she was at an incredible low and she may not have even made it through that period if it wasn't for people reaching out to her. Just a scary thought to think of her not being able to be here and entertain. She seemed like she had overcome a lot so to hear her be grateful for people in the emergency services. It was just flattering to here. I myself hadn't done as much as my brother had. He was the one more active and I was more involved with helping with fundraisers and the volunteering behind the scenes aspects but everything is a unit like that.

After talking to them for a bit she turned her attention to me. She complimented me on my outfit. She told me I looked like a little "rock star" I had the shaggy hair going and some tight ripped jeans with this rather hideous jean jacket. I don't know what I was thinking with my fashion choice there but Chyna liked it and that was all that mattered to me. I told her that I was incredibly nervous to be meeting her because I had admired her for so long. She gave me the biggest and tightest hug ever. She said to me, "You are just too damn cute, thank you for coming out and thank you for all the support over the years. I do this for you guys."

We talked for a few minutes about a variety of things. I told her that I loved that she was doing what she wanted to do and that she just looked so stunning. She was very thankful and well mannered throughout the whole thing. She said "I am having the time of my life right. I'm doing what I want to do with my life and it feels incredible to just be able to enjoy myself and some people don't get it but I'm glad that there are people out there that support me and still feel that I'm important."
I told her. "That is amazing. Fuck the haters man. You are absolutely doing amazingly right now and you look so happy and if you are having fun and it makes you feel good. I say go for it girl!"

We had a bit of banter back and forth about wrestling. I was at that point where I was just about to take a break for a bit but if I could get Chyna booked on a show then hey that would be fucking amazing! She had said she was open to doing some bookings but a lot of promotions can treat you like garbage and that they're doing you a favor by giving you a chance to "relive your glory days". I agreed with her on that. Having worked a few shows where we had some former top talent it was a mixed bag. Some of the former top guys got treated like royalty and a lot of the other ones got treated like dog shit. I don't know if it was a money making thing. If you made more money you were treated better and if you were a poor draw then they'd just walk all over you. I could see where she was coming from so I didn't want to linger on that subject for too long and changed the topic of conversation.

It felt like hours had passed when it really had only been a few minutes. The rude guy was trying to rush her through and Chyna put her hand up and told him to "give me a few more minutes, this is important." I could see that rude guy was getting frustrated so I started to try to wrap things up. We talked about a few more random things and we posed for our photo together. She was being super playful and the she goes in for a smooch on me which took me by surprise. The photo is hilarious because it looks like she is about to rip my head off. She ends up giving me a big hug and thanks me yet again and tells me to get in contact with her management and she'd let me know when she was ready to do a show and we could work out the details.

I was glad that we left on such a positive note. I was also thrilled that she kept telling the rude guy to wait a minute. It showed me that she was incredibly grateful to have a fanbase after so long and that she valued her connection to her fans. That was something that I would try to do myself as I got further in my career.

I obviously left that night with a favorable impression of Miss Chyna. I remember her making me feel at ease and that I didn't have to be nervous around her. I felt like she was a genuine person and she was interested in learning about her fans as well as just having someone glad to talk to. I could tell that she had gone through some deep shit and I wasn't aware of exactly what it all entailed. I mean that information would come out later after her passing. Although at that time I was just glad that I was able to be there and she could reach out to me to just talk. It seemed like that is something she needed. That she didn't have many real people around her and that everyone was telling her what to do and how to live her life. When we were just having a casual conversation and I was listening to her and she was listening to me it seemed like I was talking to a friend I hadn't seen in years. That is not a feeling that you get with many celebrities or people who have had some level of fame. Very rare trait.

As far as getting her to be able to do a wrestling show. It was soon after that she ended up jetting off to Japan and going over there to teach English. I wouldn't get an opportunity to meet her again until years later. I cherished the time I had and knew an appearance like this was rare so I was glad I had that opportunity. Not many people get to meet someone that they admire and that person actually turns out to be a decent person. I'm going to skip ahead a few years. This was about four years later. Sorry to jump out of the timeline here but since I am on the subject of Chyna it only makes sense to talk about the last time I met her.

My at the time husband (if you didn't know I was married you'll find more out about that in the upcoming chapters.) We had a failed move across the country. We moved down to Florida and then back up north. He wasn't a fan of Florida and he was offered a job back up north and we went where the money was. We were living in a terrible apartment at the time and about two weeks away from moving back into our old building. Our old landlord had an opening in the building. The only problem was the people who replaced us in our apartment. Another couple that we once had an awkward four-way with, the one guy was trying to keep us out of the building. He wanted to take over the entire building and run the building for some reason. He told the landlord we just had wild parties and drank all the time. The landlord knew we had a good history of paying our rent early and had to sort through the bullshit. The place we were staying at that guy was terrible. We just couldn't wait to get out of there. The sooner the new apartment was ready the better. With that in mind we were constantly looking for reasons to be out of the apartment. I saw that Chyna was coming to town to be making an appearance. She was actually doing two appearances and I thought about going to both but decided on doing the closer one.

Anyway it was a good reason to get out of the apartment and I'd get to meet Chyna once again. Little did I know that it would be the last chance I ever got to meet her so that became just as special. The line this time to meet Chyna was huge. She came out to the autograph table to a thunderous applause. The same rude guy from last time wasn't there. Some other guy was there and he was really nice for the most part. There was easily near one hundred people if not more. This wasn't going to be exactly like the last time where I got to have several minutes and a hangout session. This would be more of a quick thirty second to minute at most meet and greet. The guy taking money let my husband and I pay as one person for some reason.

They were handing out tickets because of how many people were there and just the pure chaos of it all. When they called your number you could go up to the table and pose for your photo and have your moment. Most of the people were smart enough to get in line by order of their number so it made things a bit easier. We were somewhere in the middle of the line. We were like 45 and 46 or something like that. I felt bad because she looked good on the outside but her eyes looked like she was worn out and tired. From what I was following she had an insane appearance schedule and was a bit of everywhere. Watching her interactions with other fans she seemed confused and disoriented at times. I don't know if it was too much going on or if there was any substance problems. I just felt bad and was hoping that if she was going through something that she would get through it.

It came time for our interaction. She slightly remembered meeting before. She looked at me and greeted me with a wide smile and mentioned that I looked familiar "We've met before is that right?" Chyna asked me. I replied, "Same town different place but yeah we met about 4 years ago at the club you performed, I was with my brother and my best friend." She said, "That sounds about right, that was a wild night. I'm glad you were able to come out again." We didn't have a lot of time to talk but I remember her grabbing my hand as she talked to me and just sounding so sincere and genuine. We chatted for a few seconds about her comeback. I told her "I'm glad you're coming out and doing this for fans again. You are such an amazing person. Your tour schedule seems so crazy busy. I'd need a nap for a week to recover." I was trying to think of a nice way of saying to look out for your health and don't overdo it, without seeming like a bitch. I admired this woman so I wanted to see her be happy and ok. She thanked me and said, "It's been a bit exhausting but it's nice that the people are coming out and haven't forgotten about me."

She gave me a hug, and we posed for our photo and I was on my way. I was thrilled and I was so happy. My husband looked terribly bored by the whole experience. He didn't say much of anything because he was just coming with me to have something to do and he didn't understand the importance of Chyna. Sadly that would end up being the last chance I would have to meet Chyna. Just six months later we would hear the news of her passing. I read the post on her official Facebook and thought that somebody hacked her account and was posting some fake stuff. It just so out of nowhere. I mean you thought that one day it could happen but it just seemed so unreal. I tuned into some online podcast and they were speculating on it and not aware of what was true. Information wasn't readily available and I was just crushed.

It was upsetting and I felt that I lost a close friend. Even though I didn't know her that well and only met her a handful of times, she just had that kind of impact on people. I'll always remember her in a positive way and as a source of inspiration and courage. She made a positive impact on the lives of many and left her legacy. Lots of love and respect goes out to her.

## CHAPTER 15 – I wanna be a porn star

Here we are in the year 2012 and I have no idea what the hell is going on in my life anymore. Stephen and I were split and I was getting in better shape and working to lose some weight to get more photo shoots. I really enjoyed doing nude modeling and felt so confident in how attractive my body looked. Much like Chyna, I was thinking of doing some cross overwork into adult entertainment. I had some opportunities and there was a lot going on at once and things seemed to be all over the damn place. I was on one hell of a roller coaster ride and I wasn't sure when it was stopping. Let me explain all of the shit that went down.

I had some of the best photo shoots I've had in my entire life. Of course some weren't all that good, but for the most part I was making magic. One of the photographers I worked with was suggesting that I do some videos for him. I ended up doing just a solo video. It was just set outside in the woods. It was a spin off of my sexy jungle man photo shoot that I had done previously. My outfit was already super revealing and I had to shower myself under this waterfall. It was a muggy day so the mosquitoes were out in full swing. I swear I was going to end up with Malaria or West Nile Virus by the time this shoot was over. Here I am trying to act sexy and jerk off in such miserable conditions. What was even worse is that I had a bag that had my regular clothes and shoes in it that we were carrying around. Otherwise I was walking around in a long robe like jacket. The weirdest part of it all was trying to stay turned on. There was an assistant there that was acting as a fluffer. I'd get paused in a particular pose and then have this guy suck my dick so I can be a bit more turned on. Doing a solo video was just weird to me. If I was going to do this I would need a partner. I ended up having what I considered a rather pathetic happy ending for the video. The photographer was thrilled enough with it. I told him that I couldn't work with him again unless I had someone to work with. I didn't want to sound like a diva but at the same time that was just awkward doing it solo.

I got a call a few days later and he shot with another guy that was interested in doing some video work. He saw some of my images and thought I was "hot". I mean I can't blame him! Who wouldn't think I'm the hottest thing ever? I mean am I right? Joking aside he was also rather attractive. He was a bit more of a Twink than I was. He was Twenty, blonde, and had that in between slim and slightly muscular build. I never much considered myself a twink even though at the time I borderline fit the description. Thankfully when we got together for our video this one was indoors. The theme to it was tacky as all fuck. We were playing video games on the couch and the just randomly started to make out, which would lead into some other stuff. Him and I it was all business. Before the shoot we got to know a bit more about each other and build up a chemistry but we were both interested in doing this video and then being on our way to do whatever else came across our way. I think we were both in a similar position where we wanted to get into doing adult work but we wanted to see how comfortable we were with actually doing it with someone we didn't know.

We would end up doing two videos together. The first one I got to fuck him and in the second one the roles were reversed. The second one had another lame story to it. I was home by myself and horny and I called him. The photographer basically used us as his beta test. We weren't even sure if our video would be released. After the shoot I didn't speak to the other model. We were just there doing business but I didn't much care what he did with his career. I know in some ways that sounds selfish and potentially a bad business move. I mean there was possibilities for us to do some work together on our own, but at the time I was just doing what I could to get to the next step.

I chose not to work with that photographer after that shoot. While it was nice to have some connections I felt that him not knowing what he wanted to do, wasn't ideal for me. I liked working with him, but I wanted someone who had a plan. Someone who would do a shoot and I'd know what they were planning to do next. Would this just be for a portfolio piece, were they planning on doing a gallery, art piece, or publishing a video.

I started to put myself out there with my networking. I build up my own modeling portfolio and was reaching out to photographers or video sites. I got a reply from one studio (I feel terrible I don't recall their name. I think it started with a T but don't quote me on this, I applied to a few and either got declined or no reply. I think I wasn't twinky enough for Helix, and I stood no chance getting on Sean Cody or a site like that so I was going for smaller ones) and set up an interview with them over video chat. The chat went incredibly well. They loved my look and they thought they'd be able to use me in one of their productions. They asked me if

I would be able to come to their office in New York City and I was like why not? I did exactly that. I drove myself to the train station and hopped on the train to New York the following weekend.

I got to their office and everyone was super polite and they were very smooth talking. They told me that the video chat was a prescreen and I still had to go through the actual casting process. Which would involve taking some measurements getting aroused and doing a solo. I didn't know if this was a standard procedure or if this was how it was done. This was my first time doing something with an actual studio that was somewhat well known. I had to actually schedule my casting which was not something that I knew. I had a friend that lived near the train station in New Jersey so I figured I'd be able to stay with them and just take the train back up again for the casting the next day.

I guess you could say I had an epiphany of sorts. Something was telling me that this wasn't the company that I wanted to sign with. I am not sure what made me think that. There was a ton of things that I was overlooking. Bareback was their big thing and they were talking about how they routinely test and would only stick HIV positive guys with other HIV positive guys and so on and so on. STDS wasn't something I was even thinking about when I just did my prior video. It had completely escaped my mind. I ended up calling them and thanking them for their time but declined to take anything further. It just wasn't for me at that moment.

I was beating myself up a bit over the decision but another offer would come my way. This time I had the chance to spend a few months living in the UK and doing some work there. Again this would be for adult videos. Something didn't sit right with me on that either. I am glad I listened because I found out that the guy that was trying to recruit also wanted me to be an escort. Once I heard that I was out. I had no more interest in doing anything there. At first I was excited about getting the chance to stay in the UK for a few months but who wouldn't be?

Some parts of my life seemed like they were in a downward spiral. I was just going through life with no direction. I wanted to do adult work but not as bad as I thought I did. I didn't want to do anything that would seem desperate. There were parts of me that seriously thought about being an escort for a short time for a quick way to earn money. I could pay my way through college and start saving some money for some of the things I wanted. New car, my own place to live, and things like that. I just couldn't bring myself to be that desperate. Had I really sunk that low? Was I really thinking about risking my health and my reputation? This was another situation where I am glad I listened to my instincts and didn't do it. A new opportunity to get back into doing something I loved was right around the corner. I had a glimmer of hope and a dream to chase.

# CHAPTER 16 – Gay wrestling is a thing?

I had been wanting to do a photo shoot where I was in wrestling gear for quite some time. I ended up doing an incredible shoot with a fantastic photographer. An acquaintance of mine from the one club I used to saw some of the photos from that shoot and knew that I had been comfortable being nude on camera, and was interested in doing some erotic or adult themed work. This is a point where everything seemed to fall in the right place at the right time. Not entirely but in a way and a way that it would set off quite the chain of events.

He reached out to me and was telling me about the world of erotic wrestling. I had no idea up until this point that there was a fetish devoted to wrestling. It honestly didn't surprise me but I had no idea. He was telling me he knows this guy that runs this wrestling site that is aimed towards a gay audience and features pro style matches. He told me I would be a perfect fit for it and that he could get me in contact with the guy. I was so blown away that I had no idea what to say. The next thing you know he puts me in touch with his friend and now I am talking about potentially wrestling for this gay wrestling site.

The owner of the site liked my look. He thought I had this exotic look to me and I was unique looking enough but attractive enough that I could sell matches. Now I am not going to name drop this particular company. Just know that they are Big and Gay and a direction is involved. Well the next few pages I'm going to just give my personal thoughts and feelings on what the overall audition process was like and my general experience with the company. It doesn't mean that because I feel this way about a certain subject that it makes it some sort of fact. It is just my personal opinion and be warned I am going to be honest.

I was booked on a flight and was going to be auditioning in a few weeks. In the meantime I was going to try to do as much homework as possible. I also started practicing my moves to make sure I remembered how to even take a bump and things like that. While ring rust is a very real thing, you don't quite forget how to wrestle. It all comes back to you when you get in that zone. I was checking out the company's website and I couldn't figure out how to even view their matches. It wasn't that I was stupid it was just at the time the way the website was laid out. It seemed like almost everything had to be paid for and that there wasn't even a free preview. Maybe there was and I just didn't see it? I don't know but I did what I could as far as homework went. I did manage to come across a few of their videos online that were not on the main site. I wasn't sure what to expect but from what I was watching this looked like it was a mix of wrestling and porn. Some of the matches took place in a ring and others were either on a mat or in a pool or some weird place. I wasn't sure if porn was something I would have to be doing. The erotic part of it with all the crotch rubbing didn't bother me. I just wanted to wrestle.

A few years earlier I had a chance to actually wrestle for a gay professional indy wrestling company. Pro Gay something and I can't remember quite what became of it. I know they filmed "seasons" of content. One of their wrestlers went on a rant about someone making "homophobic" comments. This guy had a character where he was all about gay rights and dressed in bright colors and called himself a gay patriot. That may have actually been his name, but I honestly don't recall. Apparently some WWE commentator said something that was deemed as "homophobic" when in reality it just wasn't. There was no malicious intent and whatever was said was typical heel commentator flare. I remember calling this particular wrestler out on it and someone claiming to be from the organization was interested in booking me to have a match with the gay patriot or whatever the hell his name was. I had sent them some samples of some of the clips I had of me wrestling. The guy also liked my look. I think the main problem was they weren't currently filming a season. That mixed with the fact that the controversy fizzled out rather quickly and what was the point of bringing me down when they have an active roster that was closer to their filming location. I can only assume that is what happened. Of course the guy who contacted me could have been full of shit and not even have worked for the company. I'll never know because nothing came of it. Anyway back to what I was saying.

I had missed out on that opportunity to wrestle for them and even though a lot of what they did was campy and not exactly the best technical skilled wrestlers. It was still wrestling and that was the part that appealed to me the most. There wasn't much for being over sexual or over erotic. Just guys that looked good and were wrestling for a gay organization. That is what was appealing about the Pro Gay whatever the hell it was called. Kind of the complete opposite of this company that I was now auditioning for. From the videos I have seen it was a lot of guys that just looked good, didn't have the best skill set, but because they were hot it didn't matter. Just to make sure we are on the same page. I am now talking about the company that I was doing the homework for and flying down to audition for.

It was finally the weekend of my audition. This would be my first visit to the Sunshine State. It was warm but it wasn't overwhelming. I got picked up from the airport and the guy running everything was very nice to me from the start. I didn't know much about him. Maybe he was in his forties or fifties. I knew he had been running the company for a while and that was about it. I knew I'd be spending my whole weekend with him and working with him throughout the weekend. He was professional and courteous for the most part. I was going to be staying for a few days so he treated me to a nice lunch. After lunch we went to the grocery story and he bought me a few meals for the following few days so I would be well fed and be able to have what I wanted to eat and drink. That was all very thoughtful. He was a rather political person and I hate politics. I don't like to discuss it and I don't like to get involved in it. Don't get me wrong I have taken part in calling my representatives, going to meetings or protests if I believed in a cause. I just wasn't there to discuss politics. I was there to do business and that is where I drew the line. I kind of just nodded as he was talking about politics and the most recent election. I wasn't going to argue because I felt like I needed this opportunity.

Here I had the chance to be on one of the most well known gay wrestling sites. I sure in hell wasn't going to blow that opportunity because of some guy's political beliefs. We got back to where I would be staying and I was shown the guest area. It was very nice and well put together. A nice little guest suite and it would be an enjoyable weekend. We got to work right away. I was exhausted from my work week. I had just worked for several days and didn't get all my days approved off for this trip but I worked as many hours as I could that week so I wasn't missing money. Plus I was a bit jet lagged from the trip. A friend dropped me off at the train station and I had taken the train to the airport. That was for a flight at seven in the morning. I had worked the night before, and didn't actually sleep because I spent all night just getting to the airport in time. I believe I took the first scheduled train at four and had just enough time to grab a bagel and make my flight.

Like I was saying we got to work right away and I was taken to a room with a ton of wrestling gear. I got to choose from a variety of gear to be photographed in. One was a longer pair of sky blue tights  and white tape wrapped around my wrists. My favorite was these silver trunks that had this snap button. They made me look more well endowed than I am. Even though I already have a decent sized package already. I had a pair of silver boots to match. The other choice was an American Flag themed singlet. My hair was messy and I looked so damn tired but pushed through this photo shoot anyway. Nearly every photo I looked miserable in. I had suggested just waiting until I was well rested but we had a full weekend ahead of things to do.

After the shoot I was mentally and physically exhausted. I didn't even eat dinner that night I just ended up passing out and sleeping the night away. The next day I was shown a bunch of classic wrestling videos that the company had produced. This would be giving me an idea of what would be going on. None of these particular videos featured the sexual side that I had seen in previous videos.

Now I was slightly confused as to if I would just be doing wrestling or I would be doing both wrestling and wrestling porn? None of this was really made clear during the process.

After seeing some of their previous work I was taken to this room to have an "audition match" to test my skill and see if I was workable with. The guy who was running the show was the guy that I would be wrestling. From what I gather he had years of experience and was larger and more muscular than I was but he wasn't fat or anything like that. He just had more bulk and I couldn't let him keep me pinned down or he would dominate me. Which is something that I hate. I absolutely hate one sided matches. Give me a good give and take and not this crap that in the gay wrestling community they call heel vs jobber. First of all they are using those terms incorrectly and that drives me nuts. In actual pro wrestling a heel is pretty much a bad guy and isn't afraid of using cheap tricks to win matches. Usually the crowd hates this guy. The guy opposite of the heel would be the face. That is the honest guy that the crowd likes and can be the underdog or the proud fighting champion. However in the gay wrestling community they seem to think Heel means the guy who is bigger and squashes and dominates the "jobber". They are big on that shit and it rather boring if you ask me.

A jobber isn't just someone getting their ass kicked. They are primary used as enhancement talent. They usually "job out" to make the other person look good. They can be a heel or face. Some of the best professional wrestlers have been jobbers and they put on amazing matches. Not just this boring squash match shit. Enough about that rant though. Where the hell was I?

I wasn't crazy about how the match went. I thought I performed well. I was incredible at selling the moves and performing a variety of moves. I showcased myself nicely. I honestly had some mixed thoughts on the match itself. He was very rough and everyone has a different style when it comes to how rough they are. I've wrestled guys that are very light holds and others who are very tight. I expressed a few times that he was being a bit on the rough side but not in a comfortable way. It didn't make me feel safe and safety is one of the most important things in a wrestling match. If you aren't working safe then I honestly don't want to work with you. If you are going to disregard the other guy's safety then you are a fucking asshole. I get being in character and being into being more dominant but there comes a point where you have to make sure you aren't going to hurt or injure the other guy.

There was one point I got put in some sort of submission hold and was then getting spanked. I tapped out because I didn't want it to go on. I felt like I was being disregarded. If I was in an actual match and discussed some "extra punishment" before hand then than is absolutely fine. I mean go at it. If it is going to sell videos I am all for it. He wanted to continue the match a bit more and deliver me a bit more punishment but I was at the point where I had just had enough. It seemed like he was into being rough and I didn't want to be that rough. I also needed to pee terribly because I hadn't used the bathroom in a while. Luckily that was going to buy me some time so I told him "Dude, I seriously need and a few of the last couple holds were a bit rough. We need to stop this for a few minutes, I'm gonna piss myself in a second and I need a breather"

I needed a moment to just collect my thoughts. I wanted this opportunity badly but at what cost? Was this really worth going through all of this? I just kept thinking on how the exposure would help me out. People would know who I was and then I could start building my brand. Who knows maybe I'd become successful and get to

240

travel the world. I sucked it up and ended up peeing and then going back. I slapped myself and got back into the proper mindset. I went in determined to do another match up and just this time I was going to match the roughness and be just as ruthless. If he wasn't going to listen to me then I was going to hit harder and be more of a dick.

The second match up I showed a bit more roughness and was taking more of his punishment and trying to fight back a bit. I figured this way at the very least I would look like I had some fighting spirit and not so easy to give up. Even though I might be stuck playing the role of the helpless jobber, I could be someone that the audience at home could root for. I was hoping that he was taking note of how I improved the second time around. I wanted this opportunity so I was going to do what I could to get it. After our match up he had a few more wrestling videos for me to watch and then we were going out for some sort of function and I was his date.

The function was some sort of political event and I didn't much know what it was about. I didn't live there nor did I care. From what I gathered someone was reelected or voted into the local office. He might have been the mayor or something. I got to meet him and had to do a fake congratulations. Thank God the event didn't last too long. We were out of there after about an hour. After we left he ran into some guy that he knew. It was one of his business partners or something and he had positive things to say about me to that guy. Things seemed like they were going well at this point. I felt like I had the job in the bag. His business partner was saying things like "Oh this is your new punk? Cute. I'd love to see him get worked over in a match." Things like that mixed with how he was responding and everything else so far made it seem like signing my contract was the next logical step.

The following day we were supposed to do some in ring work. He started having some sort of "back problems" so we weren't going to be able to do anything in the ring. That actually changed the course of plans for the next couple of days that I would be there still. Nobody was doing any work that weekend so there was nobody coming down that I could even practice with. That particular area has a huge gay wrestling scene. Easily could have found someone to be available if need be.

I was honestly skeptical of his "back problems" something just didn't sit right with me about that. It honestly seemed like some sort of excuse. He had been getting a ton of business related phone calls and was talking to his web guy about upcoming matches and things of that sort. I feel like he was overwhelmed with work that weekend and didn't have the time to devote to doing an extra match with me in the ring. I ended up jumping on Grindr and had a guy message me asking me if I was there for "wrestling". I wasn't giving him too much information because I didn't know much of what was going on. He told me he used to wrestle for the site and he was just staying nearby but would love to wrestle me if I had the time. I figured why not. I figured I could wrestle one of the former talents and if that person left on good terms then they could say positive things about me. Maybe it would increase my chances of getting picked.

He was closer to forty and he was still in rather good shape. He was a slim guy a bit shorter than I was. I think he was maybe around 5'7". He was losing some of his hair so he kept it short. We pulled out the mats and rolled around for a one on one match. Our match lasted maybe about twenty minutes. I made him submit to a modified version of the STF (stepover toehold facelock). I say modified because my step over was a bit different than the standard procedure. Might have actually altered the move and no longer been an STF. You would have to see it and use your own judgment. It wasn't something that I used in my matches often. I never considered myself to be a submission specialist by any means. I just had a few submissions I break on occasion when I'm in the mood to do a few rest holds.

We decided to have a second match but I thought it would be fun if we did it naked so I asked him how he felt about that. Of course he was all for it. I mean we were far apart enough in age that we could play some daddy and twink type of roleplay so he was all for it. We did our next match naked and that ended up in a draw. It was one of those situations that got erotic and then we forgot that we were wrestling. We ended up just fooling around instead. He said he'd put a good word in for me and he was hoping that I'd be around more often.

I had nothing else to do that night so I found Karaoke at a gay cowboy themed bar. The bar itself wasn't very packed and nobody was talking to me and nobody looked approachable. I tried to make the best of it and still have fun anyway. I sang two songs and headed back to the house. The next day was filled with nothing as well. I just ended up walking around town and exploring to see what looked interesting. I found a cute little bakery where I ended up buying random sweets. The bakery itself on the outside was decorated like a ginger bread house. I thought that was cute and random.

He took me for dinner at some traditional Irish restaurant which I enjoyed. He had received yet another phone call and this one was in regards to his "top star" and they were setting something up with him and discussing business related to him. He asked me if I knew who this person was. I said, "I'm not familiar with him and I didn't see him in any of the videos of the matches you showed me." Which was the truth. His name was something with a J and that is as much as I knew. Most of the videos he showed me were some of his older matches and some matches that looked like they were from the early 2000s or even 90s.

"I can't believe you don't know who he is? Didn't you even check out the site prior to coming here?" He asked me. I had checked out the site but I didn't see an active roster or anything of that sort. Most of the site look like it required some sort of payment or sign up and I didn't know if you needed payment to sign up and become a member. There were a few things that weren't very clear. It wasn't only me that thought that. I had asked a few friends and they were just as equally confused. Having never visited the site or not having any knowledge of the gay wrestling world before hand it was slightly confusing. I had learned a bit about web design and what was appealing and I just gave honest feedback. I don't know if my words got twisted or he just got personally offended.

Then he started talking to me about what he wanted to do with me but he had no idea what he wanted to do with me. He thought I was good at wrestling and I had an appealing look but he didn't know how he wanted to use me. He couldn't figure out how to define my character or what type of role I could play. Then he just told me he thought I was too skinny currently and that what he envisioned for me would be playing a character that had more muscle. He was saying something about how he doesn't really use guys that are too skinny. Which watching some of the previous matches I've seen one of them looked like they were having a Cheeseburger on a pole match. Like I was skinny but damn those guys looked like they were doing a Karen Carpenter cosplay. Plus one of his other top stars was this skinny blonde guy. The only reason he had abs was because he was so skinny they had no choice but to show. Then he seemed to be under the impression that I was more interested in doing sexual matches and didn't care about the wrestling aspect. Which insulted me even more because I came from a pro wrestling background. I was in love with wrestling and that absolutely was all I was interested in. Yeah the sexual side was fine but I didn't care about that at all. I'd rather wrestle. I wasn't opposed to doing the sexual things but wrestling was my first love. How can you say that to me when I spent so much time paying my dues in my local indie scene? I worked my ass off doing things that others wouldn't even want to do? Scrape the gum off the floor so my promotion didn't lose their deposit. Yeah if it helped me earn respect with my peers then I had no problem doing it.

I was a bit pissed off and thought this was such of a waste of the last four days. I also felt like I was just being lied to. I felt like he just wasn't interested and was just finding a nice way to break it to me without saying it. That actually pissed me off more. I am not sure if that is what the intention was or if he actually would have used me but either way I felt like I should have had been given an honest answer. I was disgusted by everything and didn't even finish my food. I barely spoke as he took me back to the airport.

I got on my laptop as I was waiting for my flight home and talking to my friend that had set me up. I just recall bitching about doing my best and not being good enough for this stupid shit. What made things worse was shortly after my audition he auditioned someone else who I thought was out of shape, and not even good looking. What did he have that I didn't? Why was he chosen? I didn't see the appeal. I don't mean that offensively, I just didn't get it. So he got offered the gig and I didn't. That was just salt in the wound. He's not worth mentioning his name. I'll just say his initials are T.A.

I got home and I wanted to be courteous and stay professional. I sent out a thank you card with a nice note thanking him for his generosity and hospitality. I wasn't trying to kiss ass but I knew that I wasn't going to be competing on that site anytime soon. I just like to stay professional and not burn bridges. Who knows maybe in the future something would have worked out? I knew it wouldn't so I wasn't wasting any more time on them. I wanted to move onto other things. Like I said there was no point in holding a grudge. That was not going to get me anywhere and that was not the kind of reputation that I wanted attached to me. I was bitter and hurt that it didn't work out but that is the nature of the beast. Sometimes no matter how hard you work and how hard you push, there will just be times things don't work out. This was one of those times. It didn't mean that I had to give up on the dream all together. I would just hold my head up high and push forward. I believed in myself and someone had to see potential or see my talent.

# CHAPTER 17 – UCW is calling me

I was down but not for long. I was having some issues at work because they were giving me some hell with taking some extra time off work. I went out to Karaoke at this gay bar that I went to on occasion. I was supposed to meet this guy there for a date but he stood me up so I was there by myself. I talked to a few people but nobody that was keeping my interest. The bar had copies of this gay newspaper called PGN (Philly Gay News) which is odd because we weren't close enough to Philadelphia to justify having that newspaper in our area but whatever. Something was telling me to just pick up the paper and read it. This voice in my head was not letting me ignore the paper. I'd walk by it and it seemed to have some sort of grip on me. I couldn't put it down. This isn't the most interesting newspaper so I don't normally read it but I felt like I needed to for some reason.

Maybe it would help me just block out some of the obnoxious drunks that were around me. Maybe it would distract me from the fact that I got stood up. I never expected that I would find my next opportunity. Towards the end their was an add that had this attractive guy in wrestling gear. It was an ad that was looking for wrestlers for a gay wrestling site near Philly? The guy in the ad was a guy that would later become a good friend of mine UCW wrestler Michael Hannigan. This was an ad for UCW a gay themed pro style wrestling site. They were recruiting some new talent. I ripped out the ad and put it in my pocket so I could do some research when I got home. I was over that place and wanted to get the fuck out of there. I also wanted to leave because the owner of the bar had been drinking and trying to get with me. He had followed me in the bathroom earlier and I had to push him off of me when he made some advances. He ended up trying to get with someone else and lost interest in me. I sang my karaoke song and got the fuck out of there. When I got home, I browsed the site and I was just impressed from the start. A lot of these guys were just like me. Similar builds and attractive and in their twenties. From watching some clips some of them could actually wrestle pretty well. While a lot of the guys were good looking that just wasn't all they had going for them. Unlike some other gay wrestling sites I had seen around that time.

I sent out an email with some pictures and I wasn't respecting a reply but they actually got back to me rather quickly. Michael BodySlam was the one that emailed me and told me he was interested in meeting up with me to discuss things more. I arranged to meet him and his business associate Axel. We agreed to meet at Denny's that was a halfway point between us. I wasn't sure exactly what to expect but I knew that I wasn't going to be able to eat much. I didn't want to look like a slob so I tried to order the healthiest thing I could find on the menu. At that time I wasn't eating a lot of junk food to begin with but I just didn't want to pig out on some greasy hamburger and pancake puppies. Even though that sounded delicious!

I think I ordered some egg white breakfast platter with whole wheat toast, turkey bacon, and a side of fresh fruit or something. Axel and Bodyslam were asking me questions about my wrestling experience. I didn't go into a lot of detail about my pro history because I knew they did some training. I just didn't want to sound like I was some sort of know it all and then not be able to meet their expectations. I ended up telling them that I had a bit of prior pro wrestling training and I trained for a few months but had a bit of ring rust and that I wouldn't require much training.

They discussed some things between the two of them and they both decided that they liked my look and thought I would be workable. They asked me if I had any plans and I had the entire weekend off. So they invited me to come down for the weekend to do a training session and to watch a few matches and get an idea of what they were all about. I hadn't yet signed a contract but I had a better feeling about this than I did for my previous audition.

Axel decided to ride back with me so he could give me directions in case I got lost. I had a bit of a crush on him. He was freaking adorable and he kept falling asleep. He just looked so cute dozing off. He wasn't someone I would date but I'd hang out with him for sure. We got to the UCW studio and house. The house wasn't as fancy as the other house but it was a cute house. Also they were two entirely different areas so it was to be expected that there would be some differences between the two. The studio was not attached to the house but was an old garage. The garage was actually way bigger than I expected. I loved the mat room because it had that "underground" vibe to it. Since that was part of the name it made it fitting that it had a more almost dungeon type look to it.

I met this other wrestler for the site. That would be Aron. He of course was gorgeous but for the time being gave me such a douche bag vibe. It took him a while to warm up to me but I can get into that later. I have no issues with him but I was under the impression that he didn't like me. Later he became really cool. For the time being he was a complete asshole. He just had this "I'm better than you" attitude. It was off putting.

I wasn't the only one on an audition or in the training process. There was this other newbie there. He was this eccentric guy from Alaska. He looked as odd as he acted. He had this curly frizzy hair and was shorter and not in as good as shape as I was. He wasn't fat he just was thicker. He was staying there a few weeks and training. Axel would be working with the both of us to get us ready.

I was only supposed to spend the weekend there. We were going to start training the next day. I ended up spending the next few days. Training was very similar to my previous pro training. Learning some basic bumps, lock ups, and some basic moves. We would train for an hour or two and take a break and then get back into it. The first few training sessions were almost full day events. A bit tired and sore afterwards. The only major difference aside from not being in a ring was not having to do endless amounts of squats, pushups, and situps and run around the town in the freezing cold.

After the training session and after a day of filming it was customary for the newbies to have to clean the mats. You could tell Bodyslam came from a pro wrestling background and was trying to at least instill some of the traditional pro wrestling values of respect and paying your dues into the wrestlers. Axel was very easy to work with as far as training went. He was great at giving feedback. Bodyslam was a bit more of a perfectionist and sometimes he came across as a bit more of an asshole. I'm not saying he was an asshole but I'm saying sometimes I had to bite my tongue because I wanted to say something cocky. It wasn't my place to be a cocky jerk though. This was their company, they were running the site and they were obviously successful. Just because I wanted to once and a while say "Are you fucking nuts that looked fine." Doesn't mean that it did look fine.

Alaska guy was much slower than I was as far as learning. I could tell he was struggling with a lot of things and I didn't have the best feeling about him. He was looking to do extra training during the week when nobody was  there filming, or there wasn't other people too far ahead of him. I mean I respected that he wanted to get better and put in the extra time but he just wasn't very good. He was very sluggish in some of his movements and he wasn't always the most safe. When we got to doing flip bumps, I thought he would break his neck before it was said and done.

It didn't take very long for me to get match ready. After just a few days of training I was pretty much match ready. I went home for a few days to go back to work and then during my next few days off I came back to continue my training. Alaska had some extra time between my off days but he was still not very good. I felt bad for him in some ways. He was trying his hardest but he just wasn't getting it and then he didn't realize that he wasn't very good. He was trying to move to the area and bring his sister there. Evidently his sister had some sort of medical issue and there were better doctors in the Philadelphia area. I didn't ask too many questions because it was none of my business. I think Bodyslam and Axel were starting to feel that he just wasn't going to work out.

They started to put more focus onto me and building me up. They were asking me to come up with some kind of name because they were interested in filming in their upcoming schedule because I was just about ready. Alaska was getting pissed off that they weren't yet using him. I remember him complaining and throwing a bitch fit because they weren't yet using him. He started getting a bit cocky. I suppose he was jealous that I was learning faster and I was already match ready and he wasn't. That is just the thing though. People learn and different rates and not everybody will be on the same level at the same time. It's the same way in the indy scene. There are guys that come through training and in three to six months they are ready. Others sometimes aren't ready for nearly a year. Sometimes even longer. That is just the nature of the beast!

I didn't want to get too involved in Alaska's drama because I had to focus on making sure that I knew the moves for my upcoming match. They had me practice with him and later Axel whom I'd be facing in my debut match. I don't know if Alaska was intentionally trying to mess things up or if he was just that bad. He botched the hell out of a snap suplex that I was giving him. He didn't move with me and then jumped awkwardly behind me some how. So the suplex still happened but it was mostly off time. It didn't look like one fluid move and it caused him to land awkwardly on his bump. Luckily I was protecting his head on his bump so it wasn't a total disaster. He started to complain about that and then Bodyslam placed the blame on him for not doing what he was supposed to in the move. Not sure if he noticed me protecting his head or not.

I was getting a bit frustrated with Alaska but I was staying focused because I realized that he was just being kind of bitter and I wasn't going to let him sabotage me and make me look bad. While I wasn't an ace I knew enough to at least try to make him look good, because this way I'd look good in the process. I had a few counters for some of his more sloppy moves so instead of just flat out no selling (not that I should be selling a sloppy move) I'd reverse it and then he'd have to sell the move for me. Made me look slightly better, and he was at least good at selling moves. As the practice match progressed I focused more on just giving him punishment. They already knew I could take bumps like a boss. Axel commented on my first flip bump as being "AMAZING".

After our practice match I was going to be working with Axel a bit more since I'd be working with him. Alaska didn't seem thrilled to sit back and have to watch us practice some things. I was at the point of not caring at this point. Alaska wouldn't stick around much longer anyway. Axel and I did a practice match and worked on a few things that we could try in our match. I loved working with him. He was super easy to feed off of and he was good. We just clicked and we had a good chemistry. That is super important in wrestling. The only thing I had to get used to was not being able to call out moves in advance for when we did the actual filming. That was something that we were working on while we were doing our practice match. In professional wrestling when you have a crowd you can call out moves or at least whisper them to each other. We couldn't do that here because the audience was watching from home and the camera would pick up on that.

A lot of that practice match was getting familiar with reading body language and positioning. If I was in this corner and my head is near your armpit and my arm gets placed around your neck I know a snap suplex is coming to be prepared for it. The more you do it the more it comes you you and you just know what's going on based on the position you are in. The other thing is none of us would do moves the other wasn't comfortable with or that were deemed unsafe.

Some of the other guys that were filming that weekend came over that night and were sleeping over for a full day of filming. I got to know some of

them and I instantly clicked with Michael Hannigan.
I recognized him from the ad and was thrilled to talk
to him. We were similar in a lot of ways and both
had similar passions to wrestling. I was hoping that
I'd one day get to work a match with him. This other
guy was over that night weekend. I want to say it
was Tyson The Hammer. He was a black guy
somewhere in his twenties (like most of the
wrestlers on the site so that goes without saying)
and he had an incredible body. I didn't find him
very attractive but damn his body was tight. We all
went to our sleeping quarters for the night. Sleeping
there was fun because it always felt like it was camp
or something. Sharing a room with random people
and staying up late gaming, or just chilling and
talking. Anyway I woke up in the middle of the
night and was texting a friend of mine. I was
updating her on my weekend and telling her how
excited I was about my match. As I'm texting I look
over in the next bed and Tyson is whacking off. I
have no idea if he knows I'm awake. I didn't even
know if he was awake. I get on Grindr to not only
see that I have a message from him but that he also
sent me a dick pick for some reason. I don't know if
he knew who I was or what but I just laid there and
pretended that I didn't know he was jacking off.

Watching him be filmed the next day for one of his matches all I could think of was him jacking off. I didn't say anything to him in person or on Grindr about the picture or him jacking off. I had to forget about that and focus on my match with Axel. Our match was last in the line up. I had to watch three or four other matches be filmed before mine. It would be a learning experience to help me get a better idea of what the hell was going on.

I was trying to clear my mind. I needed to get in my zone to make sure I was going to put on the best match I could and that I would be used again. I actually didn't have my official name until a few minutes before the match. Axel was going over my list of names that I had chosen. I had it narrowed down to Damien or Liam. I had always loved the name Liam and I thought it was an attractive sounding name. I was trying to come up with an erotic sounding last name to go with it but I came up blank. I loved the name Damien and at the time I had my hair dyed dark. Most people that were at the filming loved the name Liam but Axel ultimately made the final choice. That is how Damien was born.

There was some talk about me playing an anti-Axel type of role much like Damien was like the anti-Christ in the omen movies. Again I guess the dark hair made me just look more like a Damien. That idea was basically dropped because we didn't quite know how it would go over. People thought Axel and I looked alike and we could convincingly play brothers. I loved and hated that idea at the same time. I thought it was amazing because it could be an easy way to elevate me to the next level. Axel was already well established and being in a high profile ongoing feud with him would wok wonders for me. At the same time I didn't want to bring him down if it failed. He had worked hard to get where he was and I wouldn't want to be that person that stalled his momentum. Although at one point everyone gets put in a bad or disastrous story line. I also just didn't want to ride his coat tails. I wanted to carve out my own niche.

He liked Damien , because it just sounded more dirty and like a more heel name. Which is kind of the character I would be playing. I would be playing this two faced type of character. I nicknamed myself "The Image of Deception" the original idea behind the character was you weren't sure what side of me you would get. I could start off sweet and then use some dirty tactics to get my way. I also was very much into myself. I loved calling myself "flawless". So much of my mannerisms and personality was just me being the male version of WWE's group Laycool. Kind of how they acted like they were the most popular people in the world and treated everyone like dirt. Had these very fake personalities but you loved to hate them because they were charming at the same time. That is the kind of character I was going for with, Damien. That somehow managed to get slightly altered along the way but I'll get more into that in a bit.

It came time for our match and my heart was racing. I hated every part of the pre match "trash talking". I had no time to practice anything that I was going to say so I wasn't much confident in my promo cutting ability. I believe that it sounded passable at best but who would be judging that? I had to wrestle for nearly forty five minutes straight. It had been years since I had wrestled that long. I mentioned earlier about doing a match that was three hours with my best friend. That was another situation where we could at least call out moves to each other. This was me having to just hope for the best for near forty five minutes. Axel in traditional veteran form took the lead and was leading most of the match. I was mostly feeding off of him as to what I should do next and he did a wonderful job of controlling the pacing of the match. There was a point in the match where I was in control for a bit. I hit him with a move and he sold it and was out cold. Then I am jumping around begging and taunting him to get up. That was my cue of what the fuck am I doing next? I was trying to buy a few seconds. I thought to myself, now would be a good time to let him take control of the match. He was getting up and I didn't hit him with any move. Luckily he picked up on my hint and then started working me over to take control of the match. Working with him was easy and it made me look better than I was.

I wasn't a fan of having to lose my first match. I guess a rookie beating the top star in his debut match up just was a bit far-fetched. There was a reason for everything but it just annoyed me. These are the kind of things I just overthink way too much about. After the match I shook Axel's hand as any professional would do and then thought of a million ways I could have done the match differently. It was going to be filming a few more matches over the next few weeks but I wasn't sure when my first match would even debut. I knew I had to start building my brand and that was just the next logical step.

# CHAPTER 18 – Locker room drama

I knew that spreading the word and getting my name out there would be very important to my success. I knew that UCW would not do all the work. At that particular time they didn't have a huge social media presence. I felt that was something that needed to be changed. I actually had a ton of what I thought were amazing ideas. Some of which I presented and some I kept to myself. The thing was that I didn't want UCW to own something that was my idea. One of my ideas involved the wrestlers doing weekly live video chats with fans. Answering questions or hyping up the matches. Another idea I had was doing live pay per views. Do a match like normal but stream it online and since it is a pay per view format we could be a little more risque with the match. The other thing I wanted to do was set up some sort of live house cam for when the wrestlers were over that would stream online. It just didn't seem like they were interested in exploring those options so I never pushed it further.

I created some social media accounts under my wrestler name and started to follow or friend anyone who was in the gay wrestling community. I had to rely on doing a lot of my own self promotion. UCW would interview some of the guys for promos on the UCW SITE but for some reason I was never one of them. I always tried to believe there was a reason or a business strategy behind everything. I could speculate all day that someone had a beef with me or was trying to make me quit for their own personal gain but I don't have time for that shit.

I found out that my first match would be coming out and I'd be filming more around the same time. Things actually moved pretty quickly as far as that went. I decided to have a premiere preview of my match for a promotional thing. I was going to this one gay bar for karaoke and I got in contact with them to be able to do a viewing party for a preview of my match. It would be a short little preview clip of a few minutes of the match. I printed out little cards that had the link to where you could purchase and download the match. One of the other things I wanted to do was have actual download codes. Like the same concept. Instead you purchase the cards and they have a unique download code, rather than just a card with the link to the site. I wanted the download code because this way I know they would have purchased the match and I could more easily keep track of these things. I think at the time it just didn't make sense to have download codes so I wasn't going to be able to go that route.

When the match got released the viewing party was a success at least to me. I am not sure how many people bought the match after but I had people coming up to me and they felt like they were meeting a celebrity. I enjoyed it because it was getting my name out there and I was also opening up more people to the UCW brand. Something that very few of the other wrestlers even cared to do outside of their obligation to compete.

I remember filming the next two matches. One was against Eli dressed in the Black Dragon role but I can't remember who else I faced. The second match to my knowledge never made it to the site. I also don't think they stuck around. This one guy was starting training and I was instantly attracted to him. He was a nineteen year old guy and he came from a dance background. He was shorter but had a more beefy frame to him. He wasn't at all fat but he had his body frame could be misleading. Clothing made him look larger than he actually was. There were too many wrestlers there that weekend and that meant that someone would potentially have to double up and share a bed. He volunteered to sleep with me and then asked me if I would be ok with that. I'm guessing he also had a crush on me, I'll get into more of that in a minute. That weekend was rather rough for me mentally.

Everything with the exception of that guy was just getting on my nerves. I couldn't seem to focus on my match with Eli and I was fucking up. I don't recall what I did but Bodyslam got pissed off at me and we had to stop filming so he could yell at me. I wanted to so badly punch him in the face and not like a playful punch. More like a knock you the fuck out type of punch. I think I ended up putting my frustration into the match which put a little spark in my step. I just wanted to quit then and there. I was at my breaking point for some reason and I thought if I walked out now I wouldn't have to put up with such bullshit. I honestly can't remember what he was even yelling at me for. It was something very stupid, like I no sold a move or something, or I didn't sell the move long enough. I was just yelled at for giving a clothesline. I think he was pissed because I gave Eli a snapmare toss. It didn't hurt the flow of the match, that arm wasn't being worked for a while so I wouldn't have had to sell my arm being too sore. I didn't see the issue.

I finished the match and continued to be respectful to everyone in the house. It wouldn't be the last time Bodyslam would freak out or yell at me over something. I guess I was going to have to get used to him working that way. My dancer knew I was frustrated and was there to cheer me up and keep me company. I ended up going to bed that night with him and we laughed, talked, and snuggled up. I am surprised we didn't keep other people up. We somehow both woke up in the middle of the night and started kissing. Kissing led to our clothes coming off and that led to our hands exploring each other's bodies. We ended up falling asleep before even getting to any kind of climax. It was just nice to be able to feel that kind of connection with someone. It had been a while for me.

He ended up deciding that wrestling ultimately wasn't for him and he didn't stick around but we did sort of have a bit of a fling. He came around when I was wrestling to support me and also to keep me company. That would only last for a few weeks because it just started to complicate things. Some of the other wrestlers were constantly running their mouths and bothered by the fact that I'd be hanging out with him instead of them. I think I was still watching the matches and I was still participating. I don't know what the issue was. Most of the wrestlers would come and film their stuff and be gone. There was little social interaction except for a few of the regulars. We just ended up deciding that if we were going to continue to pursue a relationship of any kind that it would be best to keep it outside of the UCW grounds. I just didn't want to have people keep talking or have reasons to think I was some sort of locker room slut. I honestly liked to keep things as professional as possible so for me to even get involved with someone who I could possibly be working with professionally was just not something I would normally do. Him and I are still friends but we decided that a relationship just wasn't going to work out. I needed to keep my head in the game and focus back on wrestling.

I had two matches coming up that I was very happy about. The first being with this newcomer named Lance Thrust. He was given this gimmick of being a former porn star that was crossing over to wrestling. The funny thing was I think he actually did do porn before hand. I also think he wrestled for some other sites but I am not sure under what name. The other would be my buddy Michael Hannigan but I'll get to him in a few minutes. I ended up pitching the idea of doing a St. Patrick's Day themed match. Since I came from an Irish background and so did Lance. UCW loved doing gimmicky holiday themed matches. Previously they had just done a Santa's elves battle royal. I had a packed weekend because I had to also go on a date with some guy to see Jewel in concert. I was told we would be wrestling in kilts and wearing jock straps under them. I thought we should be wearing nothing to be honest but I was also slightly pissed off that instead of a kilt I was given a skirt.

This is the point where I was starting to feel that they were just making fun of me and just trying to insult me. I was working hard on making my character look like a legit threat and that he had a good sense of humor. I didn't like that they wanted me to be more over the top with the flamboyancy. I was protesting the skirt and said I'd go to the costume shop to get an actual kilt. Then they give me this Irish Princess tiara and I was just ready to fucking shove it up their asses. I think for the story line it was presented that Lance had switched my costume to play mind games with me. I was going to try and make the best of it.

I kept thinking that if I kept putting up with this bullshit that there would somewhere be a pay off. Whether that meant that I sign with another company, start my own video site or just be able to build my brand. I was going to let my skill do the talking at this point. Lance was actually nervous and I was excited because I was the veteran in this situation and I'd be able to carry and control the pacing of the match. That is exactly what I did and I think the results turned out well. It was one of the first times that even though I looked ridiculous that they trusted me to have some control. I carried him through the match and I made him look good in the process.

I had made a blog about him in character where I claimed I didn't like him. Truth be told he was actually a lot of fun. He impressed me with his skill and I think we had some good chemistry. He was one of my favorite people to wrestle and he was freaking hot. He needed some work yet but overall wasn't bad. There were some things that happened after the match that I never discussed until now. I mentioned in the past that he followed me around like a lost puppy. He did seem to have a strong liking to me. He was very direct and not at all shy. He just flat out asked me if I wanted to take a shower with him after our match. I didn't think anything of it. I just thought of it as two dudes taking a shower together. I actually thought he was straight so nothing sexual even crossed my mind.

We got in the shower and he asked me to set the water to my a comfortable temperature. I was in front of him and he put his hands on my shoulders and started giving me a shoulder rub. He would gently massage down my back and work his way around my hips. He started to nibble on my ear as he worked his hands towards the front of my body. He rubbed his hands over my abs and down towards my crotch. I started getting turned on and he started to rub my penis. I turned around and we were face to face. He pulled me in closer and we started to kiss. He was an amazing kisser. It was that perfect medley of passion, erotic, and intense. He started working his way down my body with his mouth until he got to my raging erection. He asked if I was alright with getting a blowjob. As I was answering with a "yes" he was working his mouth towards my cock. I didn't want to finish too soon but I was so turned on and everything felt amazing. I backed off a bit and then started to work on pleasing him. I started to suck his dick while rubbing my hands up and down his body. Doing anything with Lance felt amazing to be honest. I felt in a lot of ways that he was out of my league and way too good looking for me. For him to take charge and actually be interested in me and go after me was a much needed confidence booster. We continued to fool around in the shower and it finished with us cumming at the same time while making out. We continued to kiss as we both got soft.

He kept talking about how he wanted to keep in touch and text each other. Yet for whatever reason we didn't exchange contact info. I had assumed that we would work together in the future and there would be another opportunity. I never had another filming scheduled with him and he didn't do too many more matches after. Oh well! His loss! Moving on to Michael Hannigan.

Michael, and I had a good chemistry from the moment we met. We were similar in a lot of ways and both were one of the very few guys that UCW hired that actually cared about wrestling. A lot of guys come in and they don't have any passion. They just are there to collect that "easy money". A lot of times that makes some of their matches not look so good. Michael was different and he cared about how his matches looked and he actually wanted to be a wrestler. In a lot of ways he was living a dream. He might not have been amazing on the indy wrestling scene but in the gay wrestling world he was almost like a God.

Bodyslam, informed us that we would be in a match and Michael and I started to discuss some things that we wanted to do in the match. We shared a similar vision and we both wanted to do something special. We were both quick and had similar styles so we wanted to add some flashier moves, and just wow the people watching. We also wanted to get people interested in watching the match because I was still building a fan base and he was popular but kind of at a stand still and not getting as much promotion as some of the other guys and even the newer guys. For me I never got any promotional time of any kind. UCW just didn't promote me in the way they promoted other people. I never had feature interviews on the website, I never was shown pictures of my training as an "upcoming star" or any of that shit other people got. I knew we both had a strong social media presence so I wanted to use that to our advantage.

At the time nobody in UCW was using social media in any big way. So I came up with this idea that we would do a series of promo videos to get people interested in our match. We would trash talk each other or make fun of each other in some way. People just ate it up and it got them invested in our match. That could have ended terribly. A lot of people might have looked at it as something like me going in the business for myself and not doing what UCW told me to do. I can understand how some might think that but at the same time you have to do something to make yourself stand out. When you are sitting on the sidelines not getting much action you have to do what you can to make an impression. That is something I ended up doing.

We ended up having two matches total because the first one went over so well and UCW was actually interested in having an ongoing thing and having us do at least one more match. This was too hot of a thing to just do it as a one and done. For our second match I know we wanted to up the first one. The first one I won. Which also would mark my first win in a match on UCW. They had booked me to be on this losing streak which was something else I was frustrated about. I ended up cheating and using powder to the eyes. A vintage move but it worked. In our second match we wanted to bigger and do a few bigger spots. I remember we introduced a chair and did a few hardcore like moves. Which is something I hadn't done in years and I was not as into that but I figured I'd be willing to try it. We also did a thing where we tried to dropkick each other at the same time. We both busted out a few new moves but for whatever reason Bodyslam, kept yelling at us. He was getting angry that we were "doing too many dropkicks" and not enough "signature UCW moves, like ball grabs and crotch to face". He wasn't wrong because we were trying to make this stand out so even non UCW fans could enjoy it. We ended up switching it up mid match to the more familiar UCW style because we actually both got injured in that match. We were both very safe workers and neither one of us caused the other to be injured. I can't remember if he twisted his ankle or his back gave out in the middle of our match. I know later on he ended up having some back problems which put him on the shelf for a while. I ended up slightly pulling a muscle in my leg. Thankfully it was nothing too major but it would put me out of filming the rest of that day. I continued to work the match but if you rewatch it you may be able to see the moment it happens. He ended up winning the second match and that put an end to our rivalry.

In a lot of ways I thank him for giving me such a boost. Working with him and seeing how much passion he had and his love of wrestling made me perform better. He pushed me to my limit and beyond and we had a magical chemistry and I put

on some of my best work with him. I could never
thank him enough for such an opportunity. There
was going to be some more stuff that happened to
us but some bad timing got in the way of that.
Eventually there was a thing set up for us to actually
be a tag team. I had this idea for some tag team
scenarios even though there were no real tag teams
in UCW. Things were going alright for a while. I had
some good follow up matches and then some things
happened and it was the start of what would
become somewhat of a rocky relationship with
UCW going forward.

## CHAPTER 19 – Can't sit back & do nothing

I was riding a ridiculous high at the time. I was doing some amazing matches and I was building up my brand and my fan base. I had worked hard to get to where I was. I was my own self promoter and any opportunity to promote myself or my matches I took. I was in school for digital media at the time and I was learning a lot about design. I started to design my own little wrestling flyers and promo cards to promote some of my matches. I'd print out a few and go to the gay bars and leave some either on their bulletin board, leave some at the tables, or hand them out to people who looked like they may buy the matches.

I started also thinking of the future and other opportunities. I was in talks with the one bar to actually host a wrestling show there. I had some people in mind and I was working out some of the kinks. There were some roadblocks and things that I'd have to take responsibility for such as me not being able to sue the bar if myself or someone got injured. Seeing what kind of insurance and business things I would need if I wanted to actually go through with it. I mean it never moved beyond talks but it got the juices flowing for the future.

Around this time there was a lot of shit that was starting to go down between myself and UCW. I was presented this idea for a title run. I was told they were going to put the title on me. Even though the UCW title didn't quite mean much because there wasn't much for storylines and matches so frequently hit online out of sequence. I was honored to even be considered. I felt like in a short amount of time that I had actually made an impact. I was all for it only until I found out what the exact plan was and once I did I was insulted and felt it would have been degrading and I think they may have actually went with it with someone else but I am not sure.

The plan was for me to secure another win and at this point they didn't make me out to win all that much. I would end up being super cocky and full of myself only to lose the title about five minutes later in a ridiculous over the top goofy fashion. It would be something that was so stupid that you wouldn't believe I would lose because of something like that. I am not talking about a roll up. I am talking like a finger poke or a bitch slap kind of thing. Like....REALLY? So I told them that I was not going to do that. I just didn't feel comfortable with that idea and I didn't think it was fair to me or to my fans. I had worked hard to get where I was and that was just insulting. It was bad enough at this point that my character they kept wanting me to be more and more flamboyant and over the top. Which was so far from where I had originally wanted to take the character. The more I felt like I was improving and getting better and getting some more opportunity. The more I also felt like I was being laughed at and just being the butt of a joke.

I mysteriously got pulled from all filming that weekend. I used to stay at a friend's house that was maybe a half hour or so from the studio when it came to when I was supposed to film. I waited all weekend for a call with finalized plans. There was also a bad snow storm that weekend. I had canceled my Friday but said I could be there Saturday after the weather breaks. I showed up that Saturday and I wasn't scheduled to do anything. I just got thrown in a random match with Aron  and it was basically a squash match with him getting the win and me getting my ass kicked. I don't know if it was some kind of punishment or what the scenario. He was always kind of a dick to me but I made a really stupid joke after our match and he laughed his ass off and thought it was the funniest thing he ever heard. After that he was always nice to me and even reached out to me after I left UCW to do some work together. I just wasn't interested at that particular time. I was trying to distance myself from anyone associated with UCW.

One of the following weeks I was thrown in a match with Nick Diesel only to have the match actually canceled mid match. The two of us had absolutely no chemistry and he was a bit of a jerk to me. He wasn't very nice and he had a major attitude towards me. I have nothing against him. He just seemed to be a bit full of himself and his ability. It seemed to carry over into his matches.

I had a birthday wrestling party that I hosted at the UCW studios but in some ways this is when I felt like things were starting to get a bit more sour. I brought my then boyfriend who you guys know as Devin, to the party as my date. Later he would become my husband and then my ex husband but that is all for another chapter! At that same party I wrestled some guys some of them appeared on the UCW site once or twice and never again others were just friends that I had. One of the guys who called himself Chameleon gave me a stiff elbow to the face during our match. I had him in a waist lock from behind which I was going to set him up for a reverse bearhug into the "Flawless Face Buster". Which was basically a move where I lifted my opponent and gave them a sit down or dropped to my knees face buster from behind. Similar to the way Beth Phoenix did the Glam Slam only she did a lifted chicken wing into a face slam and I usually would go from a reverse bear hug. We had a thing where he would elbow me three times to escape the hold. They would be light enough elbow taps so that I could his elbow wouldn't actually be hitting my face. It would be the upper arm and I could turn my head in time to sell the move and make it look like I took a hard elbow to the face. Only on the third time he actually gave me a stiff elbow right to the face and whacked me in the nose which busted my nose open instantly. I continued to wrestle that day after doing some ice and making sure there was no blood. I didn't expect my nose to be swollen for a few days after.

Turns out he actually ended up slightly breaking my nose and I had to go get it realigned which I don't even want to tell you how much that sucked. Basically you get a little numbing solution and this little instrument thing they stick up your nose and then realign it from there. That was a nightmare. After the party I was trying to think of ways to make my character fresh and interesting. There were glimmers of hope of me transitioning into a more serious character. Before I could put my plan into action I had to do a custom match with this newer guy Pvt. Jack Marino. His name was a play on words because he was going to the marines outside of UCW. The guy was gorgeous all five foot five inches of him. Typical military look to him if you have never seen him and of course he had the ripped body to go with it. I didn't mind wrestling him, well or so I thought. I actually was supposed to wrestle him prior to this. It was the weekend of my second match that I was filming but for whatever reason he had some sort of last minute cancellation. He didn't take wrestling seriously and that rubbed me the wrong way. I knew the guys that just looked good and had little wrestling skill served a purpose and they drew in enough paying customers to make the company money.

The thing is though he wasn't all that bad as a performer. There was a lot of areas that he needed work on. He had a fitness background but he didn't have much in terms of a wrestling background. I was impressed that he learned quickly though. He was good at listening to instruction and then following through and delivering. Sure there were some areas he was a tad sloppy but I never got the vibe that I would be in danger with him. Since this was a custom match it wasn't going to hit the site for a while if ever because some of them can get wild. This one got slightly erotic and had specific instructions. Things such as me being in control of most of the match.

From the moment I actually met him until our match started he was whiny and complaining about a lot of things. He seemed to be very bored having to watch other matches and talking to him he just seemed like a diva. In the short time I interacted with him I learned enough about him to not like him. Then it came time for our match. We were going over some things before hand and I wanted to make sure he put on a good show so I was giving him some ideas for things he could do to me when it was his time to be in control according to the custom match script. By the way if you didn't know a custom match in UCW is when a customer pays for everything and picks the wrestlers and what happens. They pay to control everything and the wrestler's are free to decline or add revisions but once the wrestlers and customer agree a script is finalized. They were my favorite matches to do because they were the most crazy.

Our match was going well for the most part. We had a few safe words for instances where we needed to stop or pause the match. He had the match paused because he was getting pissed off that I was in control for too long. Like, really? I mean that is what the customer is paying for and what they wanted. I am following the script like what the hell are you complaining about? I had to change the course of action slightly so I could make him feel better but still be in control of the match. There was going to be a turning point where I had to kick him in the stomach while he was on all fours. I don't know exactly how it happened but I ended up giving him a stiff kick. I thought he was complaining too much about me being in control of the match. I think we had to stop for about ten minutes so he could throw a huge bitch fit over that. I didn't intend to kick him as hard as I did but it happened and while we paused filming I whispered to him "Dude, that wasn't fair to you, stiff me back and I'll sell the shit out of it." He did stiff me back somewhere later in the match and after that it seemed like he was less bitchy. Maybe that is what he needed? He needed some toughening up or something. After our match ended I went to shake his hand like I do after every match and he turned the other way. I wasn't sure what that was about but whatever I wasn't dwelling on it. There was some tension in the room and it was getting awkward. I think people could tell that we didn't like each other. He had a mini break down after the match. He wasn't sure if he would want to do another custom match after that.

In all fairness ours did get a bit erotic towards the end. I mean I got to lick him and tease him a bit. As a straight guy I can see how that would be a bit awkward. I cracked a joke. "I feel ya man, that was a twisted match. Like the person that came up with this idea was sick and twisted. Damn though! That was the best four hundred dollars I ever spent!" Everyone else in the room lost it with laughter. He even cracked a bit of a smile although he probably wouldn't admit it. I then pulled him aside and had a somewhat serious talk with him. I said, "Look, customs can be awkward to do. Regardless of if you do them or not you are going to do very well. You look great, you can actually wrestle, and the fans fucking love you. Do what's best for you man but you got that it factor so go out there and kick ass!" I may not have liked him very much but I could give him some real talk and advice. I mean he was capable of being the company's next big thing.

It was shortly after that match that I tried to go a new direction with UCW and it just wasn't working out. I was pulled from the schedule for some unknown reasons. I don't know if they just had too many matches to film with other people, or some of my matches weren't performing well on the site. It could have just been a timing or scheduling thing. Couldn't get the right person for me to have a match with and myself on the same schedule. I don't know all I could do was speculate. I decided to do this video where I had basically just put the end to my overly the top flamboyant character. I had shaved my head and I was wearing a wig in the video. I started the video by wearing a dress and a tiara. I snapped the tiara in half and then removed the wig and said I was "done being your bitch". The video got a mixed reaction. A lot of the fans I had were all for the new direction. Some of them missed my longer hair but they were curious to see where this would go.

I didn't run this by UCW so the move backfired and did nothing to advance my career or my character. It was a few months before I was put back on the match schedule. I ended up hitting my breaking point when I had a custom with Axel and I will get to that in a minute. During my few months away from UCW I was working on bulking up and adding a bit more muscle. I normally had a high cardio intense work out which helped me with my stamina and being able to wrestle for long periods of time without getting out of breath. I added some weight training to the mix and was putting on muscle weight. I was in incredible shape and didn't look as underweight as I did previously. You could actually see definition on my body. I was putting on some muscle because I thought some other companies would take interest in me. As well as me wanting to actually work for BG at that time and try to get myself more popular and out there. There was interest from some of them and some of the others but I had to turn down a few of them down for various reasons.

The one I turned down was submission based wrestling. I have no problem with that style but I did have a problem with the person who was running the promotion. I drove a few hours to go to this hotel room to audition for his site. I would be wrestling him and he would be coaching me and guiding me. He thought I was quite talented and he complimented my quickness and my speed. Which was surprising because I had just recovered from a nasty case of the stomach flu. There was something that I didn't like about him in general. He gave me a bad vibe and that sometimes is not something you want to ignore. I did some more research and when people talked about his wrestling site he was very defensive to make sure that it wasn't considered "gay" even though ninety percent of his audience was gay men. I didn't feel right potentially wrestling for a company that would be embarrassed by its primary customer base. He also just creeped me out. I didn't feel safe so I ended up telling him that I wasn't interested and was going to stick with pro wrestling.

There was another guy that tried to lure me away from UCW. He was sending me all of these business licensees that he had for his upstart wrestling company. He was from somewhere in Tennessee and wanted me to move down there to basically run the business. He allegedly had some sort of potential contract with this gay club to do shows but he needed talent. I felt like he was just looking for someone to do all the heavy work for him while he made the money. Like I could do all the hard work such as training, promoting, making flyers, finding talent, and everything that comes with being a promoter. There was no guarantee that anything would even work out. I mean his licenses and everything checked out but the risk was too high. Plus he wasn't even going to be paying for my moving expenses. Quite a few red flags there.

There was another one that took interest in me and they were based out of New Jersey I believe. They wrestled in a ring and that was the most appealing to me. It looked like it was in some sort of garage or something and they had some brown or beige sheets hung up as a back drop. It may have been called NRW but I am not quite sure. The only reason that didn't quite work out was because of their no complete clause in their contract. I didn't want to be tied down to just one company. There were a ton of guys out there that were on multiple sites. Some guys were on Rock Hard, BG, Naked Kombat, and Thunders Arena all at the same time. I may not have been interested in those sites at that time but if something came up I wouldn't want to potentially pass up an opportunity being locked into a contract.

As I was saying I ended up hitting a breaking point with UCW around the time I had to do a custom match with Axel. My boyfriend and I recently had gotten engaged and we were set to be married later that year. He had a lot of jealousy issues and hated me wrestling for UCW. I tried to get him in better shape so he could actually wrestle in UCW with me but he just wasn't committed to working out like I was. He was totally opposed to this match I had with Axel but I wanted to do it because it was going to be a good match. It ended up being a nude match and I always wanted to roll around naked with Axel so I wasn't complaining. The customer requested we both oil each other up and do a lot of rubbing up against each other. It was a hot match. We as always had good chemistry.

It was more or less some comments that were made after the match that ended up influencing my decision to leave UCW. Bodyslam mentioned to me that he didn't want to use me for a while because I was looking "chunky". Which was total bullshit because I was seriously in the best shape of my life. I had put on about ten pounds and was a solid one hundred sixty pounds but it was muscle. I still had flat abs that were slightly more defined and a puffier chest, and well toned biceps. Axel and I pretty much had similar stats around that time because he was also working out quite hard and getting bulkier. It did hurt a bit because I felt like I was making so many improvements both in my wrestling ability and the way my body looked. I ended up not being used again after that. I wanted to move onto something else and I felt that if I continued to sit around inactive I may be passing up some other opportunity.

I decided that I was going to leave UCW once and for all but I was just going to make a public announcement because there were too many people to tell individually. I made the post and talked about how I just felt there were some creative differences which there were. They wanted me to be slim like I was and not be putting on muscle as well as my character being over the top. I wanted different things. I left on what I thought were respectful terms. There was a brief shit storm right after because some people decided to run their mouths. Some other people that were talking were fueling a fire that didn't need any more fuel. It started to cause some drama and that is what I was trying to avoid.

I still stayed gracious and even thanked Bodyslam and Axel for giving me the opportunity they did when others wouldn't. I was hurt by the chunky comment but it was the nature of the business. I believe Bodyslam was just upset because I didn't go directly to him to tell him first that I was leaving. I just couldn't do a quiet exit. I needed to have some sort of closure as well as just let my fans know what was going on. It wasn't an easy decision to make but at the time it felt like it was the best move for me. I had a lot of wonderful matches and had some good exposure. I couldn't be more grateful for the opportunity I had there. I ended up making sure there were no hard feelings after and I did my best to repair that bridge because you never know what the future could hold. Plus I am not the type to hold a grudge. With me leaving UCW I found some new freedom but what the hell was I supposed to do with this new found freedom?

# **CHAPTER 20 – Now what?**

I hadn't the faintest idea as to what the hell I wanted to do next. I know I still wanted to wrestle in some capacity. I had started booking some private matches with other wrestlers even though that is something I swore off for a while because of one horrid experience. I will tell you about this one.

This was a few months before I decided to leave UCW. I met an older guy that liked to wrestle. He was more of a husky type of guy somewhere in his forties. Very hairy type of guy. I just didn't find him attractive in the way he wanted me to find him attractive. I agreed to wrestle him and that is where I was leaving it at wrestling and nothing else. We had rented some ring time and we were supposed to be having a very competitive style pro match. I agreed to doing it that way as that was the only way that I would do it. When I got to his place I wasn't feeling well. I don't know if it was because I didn't eat all day or because the flight just made me feel a little jet lagged. When I got there all I wanted to do was relax but he wanted to just wrestle the whole weekend. I only agreed to one match and that was going to be in the ring.

I agreed to wrestle him after I took a nap and was well rested. He rolled out a mat and we rolled around and exchanged a few holds. It wasn't too bad at least for that part. We were both in wrestling trunks and nothing else. He started rubbing his crotch against me which was making me uncomfortable. I told him that was something I wasn't doing because I did not agree to do anything erotic and to keep it strictly wrestling. He didn't listen and kept doing it. I just ended up submitting once he had be in a submission hold just to end the match. I just wanted it to be over and not have to deal with it. Afterwards he wanted to do some mutual jacking off which is something else I told him I wasn't interested in doing. He kept pushing the subject on me and it was just becoming awkward. I was very firm on my no because I was in a committed relationship, I didn't find him attractive and I just was there to wrestle and that was it. He got aggravated with me and ended up going in the other room to jack off while I just sat there awkwardly waiting for him to finish. The rest of the day I made plans to just avoid having to be around him. I had a photo shoot booked for later in the day and that would take my mind off some things.

The photo shoot was wonderful and I almost forgot that I was staying with that other guy. I wanted to ask the photographer if I could just stay in their spare room for the weekend but I didn't want to intrude. The next day I was back with that guy for our ring time.

We started the match and I was taking some bumps but then when I was trying to get in any kind of offense like was planned he complaining that I wasn't letting him be dominant. He said he wanted to do a total squash match and work me over which is not what we agreed to at all. He just up and decided to change it last minute thinking that I would be ok with that. It turns out I ended up having a miserable time because here I am in a ring and I can't take full advantage of it and do the things I am good at. It ended up just leaving a sour taste in my mouth and it made me not want to do any kind of private wrestling matches with other wrestlers.

After I left UCW it took me a while to ease back into the idea of wrestling with other wrestlers in a capacity where there would be no audience. That guy made me feel like he was trying to use me as an object for his desire and it just made me feel violated. I started doing some wrestling videos with my soon to be husband. At least that was someone I was comfortable with and that if it came to doing more erotic or sexual things then I would be able to. That is something I started to focus on was then just doing my own thing. I showed him a few wrestling moves and submissions that he could use and I would mostly just work him over and guide him to make him look like he could work a full match. We would have different scenarios and set ups. In one situation we would be in the living room and another one we would be in our basement which we converted into a wrestling room. I was going to order some wrestling mats so we would be able to go full into doing a few videos.

We did a series of four or five matches each with their own stipulation and we would slowly release them online. At one point I had other priorities to focus on. I was switching majors at school and wanted to start doing some stuff in the exercise field since fitness was becoming a big part of my life. I did end up getting a few various certificates in personal training and coaching so school wasn't the total waste it had seemed like. While I was working on getting my certificates we also were planning our wedding.

Once we got married it seemed to put a lot of things on hold for me. I felt like my priorities were changing and it wasn't honestly for the better. I was too focused on making my husband happy and living for him that I often put my own goals to the side. There were still things that I wanted to accomplish and get done but I ended up not doing a lot of things because they didn't meet his approval. I had finally got some wrestling mats and I was in the process of starting my own wrestling video site. I had recruited a few guys that I knew and some people that I would be able to train. It was going to be similar to what I was doing in UCW but something that would be slightly different that would give it my own spin. I planned on putting out some "free matches" in hopes of drumming up hype. The free matches were still going to be of top quality. I wasn't sure if it was the best strategy or not but it was something I wanted to test. One of the drawbacks I could see was people only watching the free matches and not paying for the regular pay matches. I thought one way to combat that would be to have "live pay per views" with some sort of tipping scale. I had some ideas but putting them into motion was the hard part.

I knew some guys through modeling connections so they were going to be some good looking guys that I was going to recruit. One of the first matches I did was actually a custom match for one of my long term fans. I worked with a guy that I knew named TJ. Tj was freaking adorable. If I wasn't married I would have dated TJ in a heartbeat. He was one of the best kissers I ever had the pleasure of kissing. I had to show him a few moves because he didn't have too much wrestling experience but he was a quick learner. I think one of the only things that he needed to work on was his selling because that was his only weak area.

TJ and I were actually asked to do Freddie Young's LRW (Living Room Wrestling). Everything was scheduled last minute but then everything fell apart last minute. There was no way that I could make the near four hour drive to get to where they were filming. I never gave Freddie a real explanation as to why we couldn't make it there. I was waiting for the final confirmation before I made the drive and I never got one. I didn't ask if I should go up there because at that point I wasn't ready to commit. I was in a rather awkward phase at that time where I was having some body image issues. I felt like I was putting on weight. The only reason I felt comfortable doing my own video was because I was wearing a singlet.

I know that sounds like a stupid reason to back out of something like that and miss out on an opportunity but it felt like the right thing to do at the time. Freddie was trying to recruit these good looking guys in their twenties. While I fit that description I felt like the revolting slob. It was the first time in a while that I had these negative body images. I also was in the process of debating on whether or not I wanted to make a move across country. I had some issues with depression and at that particular time it seemed like the area I was living in was a contributing factor. I was living in an area that was falling apart. Everything around me was closing and people close to me were constantly losing their jobs because the company they were working for just randomly closed. I had a fear of being a part of that. That mixed with the body issues I was having at the time, I just didn't want to commit to filming at Freddie's. . It sucks in some ways because it made me look like I was unreliable and I ruined my chances of doing something with him in the future.

Shortly after that my husband and I were preparing for a move across the country. I found a pro wrestling school that I could continue my training at. Things were going well until we made the move. After we moved my husband started to get a bit more on the controlling side and didn't want me going back into wrestling. He thought that either I would get hurt or if I started doing video work or running my own company that I would meet another guy and leave him. He had a lot of ignorant paranoia about those kinds of things and it put a major hold on a lot of my upcoming plans. I totally gave up on the idea of doing my own company because my husband wasn't on board with it. Looking back on it I should have just said "SCREW YOU" and did it anyway. I thought at the time working on the "perfect marriage" was a better thing to do.

Our move ended up failing because my husband was offered his old job back with a pay increase and then of course he couldn't say no. It was very hard for me to make that move after only a few short months. Later that year I would cause a controversy when some guy was creating a wrestling game featuring some of the more "popular" wrestler's in the gay wrestling scene. Guys like Ty Alexander, Ricky Roma, Tim Robbins ,and some random BG EAST guys. I made a joke about the game looking good and how they should use people with actual talent. HOLY SHIT!

Talk about a shit storm! A little joke and people started freaking out. I was getting these nasty messages and some people were taking it to a personal level and talking about my marriage and things going on in my private life. All over a fucking joke! I had nothing against any of those guys. It was mostly a jab I made in character. I guess kayfabe was really dead? I didn't think anyone would take it personally and would figure out that I was just in character. They didn't! The dust quickly settled on that for the most part but people still took it the wrong way and some people were left with a rather negative opinion on me afterwards.

Over the next few months I would keep a mostly low profile. I wasn't wrestling as much because I knew it bothered my husband and I just wanted to much for things to be well on that front. We weren't having any major problems. I mean things weren't ideal for me but I was just focusing on trying to work a steady job and help contribute. I did get the chance to do some wrestling related things and appearances.

One of my old trainers started at a new training center and asked if I was interested in helping out. On occasion I would show do some training seminars with rookies. I actually enjoyed working as a "guest trainer" because it allowed me the freedom to not have to be there all the time but also help out some upcoming talents on my local scene. I felt like I was actually putting some of the things I learned in my fitness classes to use while being a trainer so at least there was that. Even tnough I was helping train  I wanted to stay away from wrestling on my local indy scene. Sadly a lot of the old school professionalism was out the door and now things were more drama. I did manage to wrestle a few private matches, private events and fundraiser type of things. When it came to the events of fundraisers most were just one off things because they needed someone to fill out the card. I wasn't advertised and most of the time nobody knew who the hell I was and I wanted to keep it that way. As far as a live audience went I didn't want people to get invested in me or whatever character I was playing when I had no intentions of wrestling full time. Aside from that there were some gay wrestling events that I was going to go to but I've heard from other sources that they don't go very well. A lot of people who don't know what they are doing and they injure other people. I decided to avoid that hot mess.

I worked on some other things while I wasn't actively wrestling. I made my return to doing comedy. I managed to get myself booked on a few shows again until I had this awful experience. I was booked in a gay club and I don't know why but it seems that unless you are dressed in drag that gay people don't seem to appreciate male comedians. This is just something I observed from playing in a few gay clubs in my days. A lot of my material was falling flat and I know it was good material. It tested well in other places. I was used to playing in front of bikers, and blue collar types. Which is the complete opposite of what I was always able to make it work. Anyway I had this story that took place in this other club I went to and I got the name wrong and this bitch in the audience got offended because she worked there. I took the opportunity to make that into a joke too. I was like "Hold up, what is your name, sweetie?" She replied, "I'm Britney," Then I fired back, "Listen! Britney, It's a pleasure to meet you darling, I see why you work at that other club because much like that club, when it comes to people having sex with you there isn't enough alcohol that can get you drunk enough for a second visit."

I thought she would have some sort of witty comment back so I already brainstorming my next witty remark. To my surprise she got up and just walked out of the bar because she was pissed off. Then as I was continuing my story this other woman was super drunk, just came up to the stage and ripped the microphone out of my hand. She allegedly wanted her friend to come on the stage and was trying to get the crowd to get behind her because she didn't like me. The crowd sat their in awkward silence as this all went down because they didn't know what to make of it. I took the mic back and called her out on her bullshit and was about to lay a verbal smackdown on her and drag her ass through the mud for trying to embarrass me. The next thing you know the club cuts my microphone and loud music is being played. One of the owners comes and takes us both off the stage and they are dragging me to a back room. Turns out they wanted to apologize and they loved my set but didn't expect things to go that way and they didn't want to see a fight. Like, excuse me? I know how to handle people like her. This wasn't my first rodeo.

I slowly tapered off from doing comedy shows because as much as I enjoyed it I wasn't loving it. After a while the audience will know when you are just doing it just to do it and not because you love it. I just realized that it wasn't something that I wanted to do on a routine basis. Again I couldn't see myself making a career out of it, but maybe doing a few shows a year just to get the feeling of being in front of a crowd was good enough for me.

One of my friends who does plus size modeling with a gothic twist was looking for someone to go half with on a comic con table. It was for a small con but he would be selling some of his prints and I thought that was a damn good idea. Doing conventions were something I wanted to do. The only real fan interaction I would have is going to the local gay pride in a flashy singlet and hoping people would want a photo with me so I could tell them I'm a wrestler and they could buy my matches. I had ordered a few prints and little cards that had links to my social media pages. I also created this little promo video that was going to show some of my wrestling highlights with videos and pics and would just play on a silent loop. This way people would see that I was someone. We sat there for two ten hour days. Nobody that was there knew who I was and I think eight people wanted to pose for pics with me and know more about the wrestling I did.

While not a total success it gave me a taste of what I could expect if I were to do these things more often.

It is something that I will do again in the future because I liked the experience. The next few months I kept it even more low key. I ended up getting into doing some small voice acting projects. Just recording lines for small little online animations, or college students who were looking for extra voices for their class projects. I always loved acting so this was a fun way for me to discover something else that I also loved doing. The plus side was I didn't have to look a certain way to get a part. I could just rely on my voice to do the work! While I was doing things to finally make myself happy and things that I enjoyed. It seemed like my husband just didn't seem too proud of me. I think he had a different idea of what I should be doing with my life. I mean I was working and also doing things I enjoyed but I think he had different expectations for our life. This next chapter is where things get a bit complicated but it surprisingly ties everything together in some twisted way.

# <u>CHAPTER 21 – Starting over</u>

This has been one hell of a rowdy roller coaster of a journey that I have shared with you so far and this train just keeps on rolling. When I was writing this there was a lot that I debated on putting in the book. I'm telling you this whole project took way longer than I ever thought it would. When I first decided to do this I thought I could easily have it done in just a month. Sharing this story with all of you have been surprisingly therapeutic. It also has been rattling my brain a bit. There were times that I had writer's block or there were times that I was just like "FUCK THIS! WHO WILL READ THIS SHIT?". I'm glad I stuck with it. There were some things that were hard to write about throughout but I felt like I needed to get out so they weren't bottled up anymore. This is going to be one of those chapters so I give you a warning now.

When 2017 came by my life was just in shambles. Things were slowly falling apart in my marriage but I just didn't quite realize it yet. We argued a lot and it seemed to be a more regular thing. We used to go a few months and then have some sort of big argument and blow off some steam but it was turning into every few weeks. I wanted to go back and finish school to some capacity. I was working two jobs and the one I was trying to get transferred closer to where I lived because the drive was just becoming to be a hassle.

I believe married life made some of my issues that I had with depression and anxiety a lot worse than they ever were. It is hard to explain why I felt that way. I was of course at the time in a happy place because I was with the person that I thought I was meant to be with. Yet I constantly felt tied down because I couldn't do the things I wanted to do with my life because I had to be living to make someone else happy. A lot of his family just flat out did not like me. They would pretend they would in a lot of situations but I always felt some tension or that I was the topic of conversation when I left the room. There were days that I would wake up and I would be crying for no reason and then things would get worse when I would have to deal with the drama his family was bringing. There were days I called off work because I'd wake up with a pounding headache or I just couldn't get the motivation to get out of bed to go to work. I would just grab a stuffed animal or a pillow and just not move and lay there feeling apathetic. I wanted to get some kind of help so I wouldn't one day just do something stupid to myself.

I found myself going out to the bars a lot even though I wasn't a social person. I didn't much drink although I would have an occasional mixed drink. Karaoke was my go to thing. Just getting out of the house and being able to sing a song that I could relate to in front of a crowd of people, somehow got a lot of things off my mind. I would go out for days in a row and then I would just cut off communication with everyone around me. I had this cycle of having fun and then going into hermit mode and letting my thoughts consume me.

I wanted to get some help but the idea of being on any kind of anti depression medication scared me. I would frequently think of Chyna and her situation and how different prescription medications ended her life. I didn't want to ever be in that situation where I was that out of control. I had a short bout of depression for a few weeks and then all of a sudden everything was better. There was no apparent reason. Things just felt amazing again. During this period I started to surround myself with my close family and friends and I think it was me internally knowing that I was going to have to depend on these people in the near future. We just had incredible bonding experiences of just drinking beers around a campfire, sharing funny stories and memories. Right around Easter time was when I was escaping to these people the most. I ended up having to go to the hospital for what was a suspected seizure.

I ended up being fine but I did have an incredibly nasty sinus infection that needed to get cleared up. My husband's dad was married to a guy. There was this whole thing where he tried to buy his way back into my husband's life. They didn't have the best relationship but his dad started to shower him with gifts and expensive things. His dad's husband sent me a text message criticizing my husband for taking me to the hospital. In response I just said, "Thanks for your concern but I'm not in the mood to argue with anyone. I'm enjoying a lovely dinner with my family and I hope you are as well. Have a good Easter.". For one reason or another he started going off on me and saying that my husband had worse health issues and I was selfish. Then he randomly started telling me what a loser I was and that my job wasn't good enough to support him.

I blocked him that moment because I just wasn't dealing with the drama. I didn't need to defend myself for working two jobs. They were both for good companies and they were much better paying compared to some of the similar jobs in my area. My husband was bothered by all of that for about two days and then started talking to them again. He was enjoying a lot of the free shit he was getting so I suppose it would have been stupid to cut that out of his life. Things seemed to be alright between us for the next couple of months but by the time mid summer rolled around things were about to change.

My husband left for a business trip for his job. He was going to be gone for two weeks and we both would be alone. This was the first time in our entire marriage that we got to have that much alone time. I wasn't even sure what the hell to do with myself during that period. I had a few friends come over so I wouldn't be completely bored and I mostly started to clean. I felt like every action that I decided to make during that time was a premonition of things to come. I didn't quite know what it was yet but I had a feeling something big was going to be happening. I started decluttering our apartment. I was throwing out things that we had no use for anymore or that we were never going to use. Some of these were things that I bought at storage and pallet auctions and hopes of reselling. It was just shit that I couldn't get rid of if I tried.

In the middle of all of that going on I just had a break down for some reason. I wasn't feeling good at all and I just started crying. I went to the bathroom and was going through the medicine cabinet and there was a bottle of sleeping pills in there. I stood there and I stared at that bottle. I started questioning many facets of my life and where I was at. I debated on if I should take any of the pills just to knock myself out for a bit so I wouldn't have to question anything. I don't even know where the hell the bottle came from. I think a friend of mine left them here when he stayed over for a few days. In the back of my mind I knew that I also had alcohol in the house. I started to try to do the math in my head of what combination of pills and shots that I could take that wouldn't kill me but severely knock me out for a while. I had no idea what the hell I was thinking or how any of that would make sense. I knew I couldn't do anything alone and being alone at that particular moment was not something that should be happening.

I called a friend of mine and I told him that I needed him to come over right away. Normally he would question it but I think he heard the urgency in my voice and didn't ask questions. He had a key to my apartment and let himself in. He found me just sitting on the bathroom floor with this bottle of pills. He saw just how drained and pale I looked and took the pills off of me and just let me cry on his shoulder. I started to think of all of the things I needed to stick around for and how many people need me in their life. I had hit a breaking point. It was the worst I had ever been. My friend helped me through that night. He took the pills off of me and monitored my behavior to make sure I wasn't suffering from any side effects of the medication. He wasn't sure if I took any or not. I hadn't at that point. He poured out the bottle and counted how many were in there vs how many should have been in there. He believed me when I told him I didn't take any because I honestly hadn't but he wanted to make sure anyway. He then went into the kitchen and poured any of the alcohol I had in the house down the drain. He stayed with me the rest of the night to make sure I was alright. I woke up that morning to a fresh cooked breakfast and felt like nothing outrageous had happened the night before. I felt better than ever. I rejuvenated and that I was ready to take on the world.

A few days later my husband was due to be coming home. He messaged me saying that he was on his way home but was stopping at his dad's house. I was a bit pissed off about that because he hadn't seen me in two weeks and he would be passing our apartment anyway to get to his dad's house. So him completely skipping over stopping in to say hi to me or unpack his stuff seemed odd but I didn't dwell on it. He kept messaging me saying that he would be home in a little bit. Hours passed and then he just stopped replying. I tried to get a hold of him to see what was going on. I had plans the following day and needed to see my family and here he had the car. We never got a replacement when my car finally broke down after being in my family for fifteen years. A couple of days had passed after he was supposed to be home. I was talking with my best friend about everything that was going on. He thought things were odd too. We were joking that he might not be coming back. Sure enough after we were joking about it he finally texted me just saying that he wanted a divorce and nothing else. It was such a shitty way to tell someone that you wanted to end your marriage. He said he'd be by to pick up some of his stuff.

I kept my cool because deep down I knew that this was what I wanted as well. I was thinking about doing it but I was going to do it a bit differently. Mine was going to be face to face but when the time was right. I wanted to be somewhere warmer by the end of the year so I wouldn't have to deal with another brutal winter. I just needed more time to get myself together and save up some money so I could do things properly and not be a burden. Well he threw that idea right out the window and did it in a shitty way. He came by and picked up some stuff and said that he'd be staying with his dad until I decided what I wanted to do. Basically he was telling me "If you decide to stay in this apartment I'm gonna live with my dad." I didn't want to stay in that apartment. I could have just to prove a point. I wanted to be in a house and not an apartment and I also just wanted to get the fuck out of the area we were living in. The area was just going to shit everywhere you looked. I wanted to get out of the area all together. When he picked up his stuff he took the most random shit with him to his dad's. He took these fucking light sabers. Like I was going to throw out a one hundred and fifty dollar light saber or be spiteful and sell it? Like what the fuck kind of person did he think I was? I told him that I would be moving. He agreed to let me keep some of my stuff there for a couple of months because I couldn't afford a moving truck at the time. Turns out his sister decided to come over and throw all my shit away after I had moved out. Thankfully I didn't leave anything of too much value there. I mostly had some household decor and bigger things that I couldn't fit in a car.

I was glad that I was working at the time and was able to be able to afford to move and on such short notice. I wanted to try hard to remain friends because I had no bitter feelings but the way he handled things made it nearly impossible. I feel like I had wasted nearly five years of my life by being with him. There were so many things that I felt I should have done and went after. I felt trapped and had we stayed together things probably would have been worse.. I needed to be bigger than all of this and move on. It took me a while to process things. People around me were shocked how well I was holding up because that is a devastating thing to go through. My job was nice enough to give me a leave of absence. Right before all of that I was at the lowest I had ever been in my life. If I could survive that whole ordeal then this was nothing in comparison. If that didn't break me then he sure in hell wasn't going to.

The following months would be a huge test for me. I couldn't believe how much I ended up just getting content with settling and not doing the things that I wanted to do with my life. In a lot of ways I would have so much to rebuild. I forgot what it was like to go out and go on dates with people. I forgot what it was like to just not have to tell someone what my every move was and that I could just do what I had wanted. I was enjoying my new found freedom. I couldn't believe how much the quality of my overall life was improving. I was losing weight that I had gained during my marriage. My stress levels and the amounts of headaches I was getting were reduced. I was able to manage my depression and not feel like I was being judged for it. I still had some issues with anxiety but being in a new place and having to start over contributed to that. Once I got more familiar with my surroundings and got over some of my initial fears that came with that, I was making new friends and enjoying life.

I have nothing against him. I don't hold a grudge. Nothing I write here is meant to make him look like a bad person. He isn't a bad person by any stretch of the imagination. There was a period of time where he took care of me and was one of the most loving people I had ever met. He just long term wasn't the one for me and that is alright. People are sometimes brought into our lives for certain reasons. Sometimes we have to fail to become better people. Sometimes we have to fall down and start over to see some improvements in our life. Just like in the wrestling world. Nobody starts out as an amazing wrestler. Sure you might have some natural ability or be talented in some areas but at the end of the day you have to pay your dues and put in the work. Sometimes you will struggle and you will want to give up. There will be days when it feels like hell. There will be times you wonder what the hell you are even doing it for? At the end of the day you keep going because you have that drive and passion. It is a spectacular feeling indeed.

It feels like this is a good time to bring this chapter as well as the entire book to a finish. I've enjoyed sharing my personal story with you. I've had some amazing opportunity in my life and I've had the chance to do things that I never thought I'd be able to do. Every expectation I ever set for my life I exceeded. I can never thank everyone enough for the opportunities I had and the successes I found. There's just so many people, from the trainers who worked with me, the teachers I had, the fans who believed in me and supported me and pushed hard for me to be featured in matches. I would not have enough time to list everyone but thank you to everyone. To me the best thing to ever happen to me was just having the opportunity to entertain. To be that person that maybe someone somewhere in the world they look at me and think, "He's just like me. If he can do that, then I can do that!".

I'm not saying that I need that admiration because I don't. It is always just a nice feeling to have if I can give someone a bit of inspiration or hope to do the things they want to do with their life and not be afraid. I know there are people out there who are proud of me for the things I've accomplished and you know what I am damn proud of myself as well. So with all that being said it is best for me to put this book to a close. As I do just remember......."STAY FLAWLESS!"

Made in the USA
Lexington, KY
11 May 2018